Walking Out of **Darkness**

STEPHEN SHAFER

WESTBOW
PRESS
A DIVISION OF THOMAS NELSON

All Scripture is taken from Archaeological Study Bible NIV version Published by Zondervan Corp., 2005. Grand Rapids Michigan 49530 USA

WestBow Press books may be ordered through booksellers or by contacting:

WestBow Press
A Division of Thomas Nelson
1663 Liberty Drive
Bloomington, IN 47403
www.westbowpress.com
1-(866) 928-1240

ISBN: 978-1-4497-1360-7 (sc)
ISBN: 978-1-4497-1361-4 (dj)
ISBN: 978-1-4497-1359-1 (e)

Library of Congress Control Number: 2011923942

Printed in the United States of America

WestBow Press rev. date: 02/25/2011

To Mary Hatton, who always said I should do this.

You were my guiding light and my angel in the darkness.

You were my voice of reason, and you let
me know whenever I made a mistake.

No matter what, you were always honest and loving.

You saved my life!

Thank you. I love you.

Contents

Acknowledgments

I would like to thank Jesus Christ for keeping me alive long enough to write this book, and especially for walking with me through the turmoil. Second, I would like to thank my wife, for allowing me the space to write, and my family, for supporting me through the process. I would also like to thank Pastor Bob and Sue Misiak, for teaching me how to wait on the Lord and for reminding me that everything is about relationships. Thanks also to Kathleen Perry for her editorial support. To Louise Michowski and Sue Obaza and family, and to the person who wishes to remain anonymous: thanks for your financial support; without it, this book would have never been.

Introduction

People write for a lot of reasons. Some write to entertain, some to inform, and some to persuade. I write in hopes of reaching people where they are, perhaps helping them through a challenging time by empowering them to turn to solutions other than the usual ones.

There is a certain comfort that comes from talking to someone who has been through what you have. This is not to say that someone who has only book knowledge—that is, someone who has only heard about what you are going through, but has never experienced it—cannot help. Empathy allows us to identify with others who have experienced things that we have not. At the same time, there is no substitute for the real thing. You gain a personal perspective of an incident once you have experienced it. As a result, camaraderie forms among people who have been through the same types of things.

And for those who have a past like mine, everything in life is performance-based. Ideas such as love, peace, hope, faith, and unmerited favor, as well as grace, seem foreign. In fact, as I write this book, I am still seeking release from my past. But my past and the feelings I have about it are slowly being re-arranged, so that instead of relying on works or performance to measure my worth, I rely on those famous three: grace, mercy, and love.

What I am saying is that, as you read this book, try to *identify* with my experiences, rather than to *compare* them with yours. I realize how difficult life is. But now, I also realize that there are many paths that lead to the place where you feel like you've "made it," and this is the message that I would like to pass along to you. You see, when you have spent a life searching for something, but never quite reaching it, it does something to you. And we, who are left wanting, who feel as though there is something more or something missing in our lives, want to know the answer to our questions. This book seeks to explore those subtle questions, and to, I hope, provide answers for those of you, like me, who are continually seeking more.

So, search these pages for answers that will allow you to get the relief that you so want and need, but know that I only have the answers because of Christ's love. I am living proof that there is no saving someone without the hand of God. I was once one of those folks who told you right up front that he didn't like himself, have goals or dreams, or hold hope for the future. But I can tell you firsthand that change is possible, that if we decide we no longer want to be miserable, angry, hostile, fearful, resentful, self-hating, and hateful of others, we can overcome those feelings—those old "tapes" that play back in our heads. Also know that by *change*, I do not mean small, inconsequential differences, but life-altering, mind-boggling, intense alterations that switch everything in life from negative to positive. Of course, that kind of change doesn't happen overnight. It happens over time, with hard work and at the hand of God. But then, nothing worthwhile comes easily.

I have no magical cure, no special pill, no certain procedure that guarantees success, but I do have Jesus Christ as my personal savior and his Holy Spirit living within me. Listening and being sensitive to the prompting of that Spirit and being guided by the Word of God have changed my life and allowed me to be the person I am today.

Change is a process. It has taken prayer, dedication, a willingness to change, and finally doing what I was told. It took me listening to another who knew more than I did. And, most important, it took finally giving in to a higher power, releasing all my preconceived notions of who Jesus was, and trying to find out who He really is.

I have wanted to quit several times, just today alone, as this journey has been the hardest I have ever taken. But, I am gaining insight and revelation, and I am becoming the person I always wanted to be. I have feelings today. I can cry today. I can see someone in need and want to help today. I am no longer filled with hate, envy, malice, fear, and resentment. I am no longer perpetually angry. I have been delivered from myself.

This is the story of my journey, from start to finish. I am still not the person I want to be, but I am not the person I was either.

One: **A Rough Beginning**

My story starts at one of those times in life when you reach a turning point in the road and have to decide whether to keep going the way you always have or to leave your comfort zone, drop the game, and head off toward the unknown. But to understand that story, you must hear another one. We must back up to the very beginning of the road that I was already on, to see how I got there in the first place.

My childhood memories are sketchy at best. I have also learned that I have blocked out a very large part of my past, as well, as a defense mechanism. They are segmented, fractioned, and incomplete. Certain moments stand out, however, and more of them continue to pop up anew. I remember, at the age of two, riding down some cement steps after watching a daredevil on TV. I remember a giant turtle living under our grill in the backyard. I remember an Aunt always being there for me, and my mother that was very abusive.

As it turned out, I was no more out of control than any other child. My issue was that from two years of age on, it appeared to me that I was not really wanted and that I was always in the wrong. I can remember being punished a lot of the time during the time I lived with my mother. I can remember her being very angry, and that anger being taken out on me.

To add to the turmoil, my mother and I moved each year or so from the time I was five until I was fourteen. This made life hard because there was never any stability for me. To this day, I have no roots to speak of, although I can identify with growing up in northern New Jersey.

It was impossible to make long-term friends. I was always the new kid, always the one having to prove myself, and of course, nothing but trouble ever came of that. There was always fighting, and, until I was twelve, I would always lose because I would not fight back. I would just stand there and take it. After all, that was what I knew. At home, you just stood there and took it, so I figured it was like that everywhere.

Besides, all through grammar school, I was bigger than everyone else. I figured I would really hurt someone if I hauled off and hit him, so fighting didn't even seem like an option. To boot, I had no male role model at home to teach me how to stand up for myself, and I had been taught in church that you turned the other cheek and went out of your way not to displease God. Of course, none of this bade well for me; when kids know they can use you as a punching bag, you tend to get picked on a lot.

I grew up in Pentecostal churches, and at that time their doctrine was "no fun." No dancing, no listening to rock-and-roll—in fact, no listening to music at all unless it was psalms and hymns—no playing cards, and no going to movies. I learned to be frightened of God. The God I was taught about as a youngster was a God who was just waiting to punish you, and itching to hurt you. I never picked up anything about grace, mercy, or love. It was all just rules and regulations. I often heard things like, "You had better behave. You do not want to burn in hell, do you?" and, of course, the ever-famous "What if Jesus came back right now? Would you want Him catching you doing that?" Life with Christ was always about performance and punishment, and it all appeared very rigid to me.

It did not help that as I got older, I noticed that many people appeared to be hypocrites. Almost daily, I would see people in the community who acted all pious in church every Sunday behaving like the rest of us during the week. That did not add up to me, but I figured all Christians were like that. As a result, I was completely turned off by any form of Christianity, and that led to my rebellion, which has taken the better part of the last twenty-five years to overcome. I have been walking with Christ now for six and a half years, instead of Him having to drag me everywhere we went. I can honestly state that I am finally in relationship with Him now, and that my life is fully dedicated to Him. Yes, I still sin, but today that is a mistake, where when I lived in sin I would screw up once in a while and do something right. Now I will screw up and do something wrong, and I know that I can repent and start over today, without condemnation.

Back then, demons were also quite the fashion. Any symptom you could not identify as being part of a specific disease was on a list distributed by the Pentecostal churches and said to be a symptom of demonic possession. There were both physical and mental symptoms—things like ringing in the ears, constant headaches, uneasy feelings, an inability to concentrate, misbehavior, and disobedience to parents, and if you displayed any of them, you were prayed for and exorcised by the deacons and pastors. This, of course, happened to me numerous times and at numerous churches, since my mother would always tell anyone who would listen how terrible my behavior was. Once, when I was eleven or twelve, we were going to a home-church. The people heading it up were very rich, and they had a daughter who was around my age and very beautiful. An evangelist came one summer day, and everyone was going swimming in the in-ground pool in the backyard. I, however, was not allowed in. Instead, my mother, who had been talking to the evangelist, both got together with the deacons. They all sat me in a circle and prayed over me, demanding that whatever was in me come out. When they were done, they all clapped, after which I was allowed into the pool, and around their daughter. As far as I could tell, nothing happened, which taught me at an early age that Christianity was a performance art.

As my mother believed in the church doctrine of "spare the rod, spoil the child," I also remember getting physically punished for getting unsatisfactory marks on my report card for "Behavior," "Listens in Class," and "Plays Well with Others." I failed all of these areas throughout my entire scholastic career, which meant whenever the report card came home, I knew I was in for punishment

It wasn't just on report-card days either. I was always the one getting notes sent home saying I'd been in trouble for talking, looking out the window, having too much energy, or acting impulsively. Not a week went by that something did not get sent home, so I was being punished all the time.

As I look back on my behavior, I realize that I was a hyper kid. I did not have a dad, and my mom was working all the time, so I was left with all this unmanaged energy, which ended up coming out sideways, mostly as my just plain running wild. I was just full of energy, full of life, and my mother was not equipped to deal with that kind of kid. I truly think that she did not realize how traumatic she made my life. To her, she was just disciplining a hyperactive, overzealous kid who would not do what he was told, yet to me, it filled my life with nothing but punishment.

I must also add that I have grown to realize that my mother did the best she could with what she had—and what she had was a lot of issues, which she took out on me. All of us try to do the best with what we have, but, unfortunately, with kids, that is sometimes not enough, so we must reach out to others for help and information. Children are very moldable, very impressionable.

If you program a kid to think that he is nothing but wrong because he is always in trouble, and you keep putting unrealistic goals in front of him, the result will be a very angry, hostile, and extremely unforgiving kid who wants to get that hurt out anyway he can; and acting out is a way to do that. How? There comes a time when you start to believe that you *are* no good, that you are never going to change, that you will be in trouble all your life, so what is the use of trying? Why even try to get help if it's never going to work? Why go all out and do your best only to have it be wrong again?

I actually remember this attitude setting in at around age ten, at which point, I stopped trying. I expected to get punished and to be told I was no good regardless of what I did; no effort, however big, would help me measure up. I learned that negative attention was at least attention, and that you could get into the spotlight a number of ways—so I became the class clown, the reject, and the outcast, as it brought with it as many accolades as being prim and proper. I became the kid your mother warned you about before you left the house.

I did have an Aunt who was my mother's roommate for the first seven or eight years of my life. She always seemed to be available for me. She was like a second mother. When I turned nine or ten, however, she left the country to be a missionary and never came back. After she left, there was no buffer between my mother and me, so the physical punishments became even more severe.

Had I been a girl, I think things would have gone differently, but that was not to be. You see, my mother was always taking in foster children up to the age of ten or so, there were at least one or more children in the home besides me.Of course, I ended up resenting them, and that was not their fault, but at that tender age, from the time I was six to about ten, I did not know the difference. So, I spent most of my days resentful. I began to dream about being given up for adoption or sent to another home I just knew that if it ever happened, I would be better. Unfortunately, by the time that dream came true, the damage had already been done. I was too far gone for another home to help.

Two: Change

At the age of twelve, while getting punished I snapped. I took all the punishment I was going to take. And with that, I felt a power awaken within. I was no longer scared—of her or anyone else. I was no longer going to just take what other people were dishing out. I was going to stand up for myself. I had taken all the punishment I was going to ever.

Now in the sixth grade, I stopped allowing the other kids to pick on me, and that surprised some people, as they got themselves hurt. After getting beaten up at school almost on a daily basis, and at home almost as often, all of a sudden, things changed. Things went downhill from then on. I never did finish the sixth grade, and I never did go back home for any length of time, but I also never got beaten down again without fighting back.

Soon after, my mother heard about this farm that some kids from the church were going to for a few weeks to get experience working on a farm—you know, to get away from the city, learn another life, see the country, and supposedly learn about God at the same time. Unfortunately for me, there was a lot more going on at that farm than anyone knew. The man who ran it was a captain in the Army Reserves and a chaplain. He was also a child molester, a pervert, and a pig. As far as I knew, he tried to touch, molest, hurt, or engage in sexual acts with everyone who came to his farm, whether male or female, and I am pretty sure that included his own kids.

This was my first experience with a scumbag, but it would not be my last. At the beginning, he was nice, but as time went on, he would try to do little things that appeared weird, but you could not really say how, until finally he outright tried something. When it happened to me, all hell broke loose. I found myself fighting for my life and my sexuality, as he tried many times to fondle me. And then as time went on and I continued fighting back, he turned to brute force, which was when I learned to sleep with my back toward the wall, with one eye open, and a weapon at my side. Eventually, I moved myself and my stuff out of the house and into the barn, just to be away from him. Although it always smelled of cows, which always made me smell like cows, at least I had a door that locked, and I had a wood stove and a dresser.

It was about nine months before I was rescued from that place, even after repeated phone calls to my mother in which I would plead for her to come get me. Each time, she would speak to him, and he would say everything was fine, so she would leave me there. During one of these phone calls, at the very beginning, she actually enrolled me into a school there for half a year, so I could live there longer. I did not fit in at that school, either—smelling like cows doesn't make it easy to find friends— which added misery to an already bad situation.

I do have to say, however, that even while I was there, even while fighting to keep from being raped, I knew that God was with me. One instance, I will never forget. During the summer, there were others around besides his family, as he had gone to numerous churches to get kids to come and experience the farm life, so he would schedule bonfires, hiking, games, and farm chores for us (as it was a working farm). This particular night, after he had read to us from the Bible about how the voice of God was like a mighty, rushing wind, and how God was always with us, no matter what was going on, he took us to the top of the largest hill on his farm; All was quiet, as we just sat and listened.

Suddenly, there was the sound of a mighty, rushing wind, like the one he had just read about. But the strange thing was, there was no wind. We looked around, trying to figure out what could have made the noise, but among the wide open spaces of the hay fields, it was clear that there was nothing but us for miles. From that time on, I have always said that I once heard the voice of God.

Things got worse at the end of the summer, after all the other kids went back home. The only "friends" I had left were from across the street, and they were twice as old as I was and into partying all the time. They thought it was funny to get the little kid drunk or stoned—and so, I was introduced to partying.

As this is part of my past that my mind has forgotten as a defense mechanism, I don't remember exactly what all happened during this time. I do know that things were just plain bad all the time, until the one day my mother showed up with a few others. When they saw how I was living and where I was sleeping, they took me and my stuff out of there. For that, I will always be grateful.

A few years ago, I heard that someone had told on him, as others of us had done, but this time, someone finally listened. He was brought up on charges—a lot them—as people kept coming forward, but I have to say I was not one of them. I do not know what happened to him after that, although I heard that he committed suicide.

And so as I was taken from the farm to a house that was to be my home for the next six to nine months, change, as it does in every life, happened again. The thing with change, though, is that its outcome depends on how we deal with the change. In other words, the outcome, good or bad, depends on the choices we make. Choice is the key; it is given to us so that we can either destroy or make something of ourselves. And it all stems from Adam. Adam was given a choice. He could have spoken up to the serpent, called God, and had the serpent thrown out of the garden. Or, he could have thrown the serpent out himself; after all, he had dominion and authority over the creative process. But Adam did neither of these things. He just shut his mouth and went along with his wife as she was being deceived. Thus, God had no choice but to do what he did. He could not allow them to eat of the fruit of eternal life, or there would have been no chance of redemption. God had to do what he did because of the choices that Adam and Eve made. I say this because I, too, had choices, and I made bad ones—and particularly during this next phase of my life.

The people I was placed with were good, Christian, Spirit-filled believers. The only problem was me. That's not to say I didn't enjoy my time at my new home. Now thirteen and having just been introduced to partying, I was more than glad to re-acquaint myself with civilization and to become a normal kid again. I was back in a city, back around people who rode in cars instead of tractors, and I was actually happy. The people who took me in gave me my own room and full run of the house, and they treated me like I was part of the family. They let me go to school functions, listen to music, and go to friends' homes, and the only real conditions were that I go to church, be involved at school, stay out of trouble, and obey a few simple house rules.

They really did try to get me back to being somewhat of a good kid, but the damage had already done too much. After what had happened to me—what I had been through with other believers and what had been done to me in the name of God—I wanted nothing to do with other so-called Christians, and even less to do with God. I was more interested in smoking, drinking, girls, and drugs. So as the family kept catching me breaking their few rules, such as when I smoked (which I began to do constantly) and snuck out to parties, they got fed up. They tried casting things out of me, they tried counseling, they tried punishment, but I was too far gone at that point for anything to work.

We all hate change. Oh, some of us may say that we love it, that we look forward to it, that it is what keeps us going and keeps things fresh, but the bottom line is that we usually feel terrified when it comes. We are struck dumb over change. The undeniable fact, however, is that change *will* come, and with it will come a newness—and it is this newness that we crave. It's what really does keep us going. You see, newness is what keeps life worth living. Think about it. Whenever you get something new, what is your reaction? You get all happy inside, like a kid at Christmas. And who doesn't want to keep that feeling alive for as long as possible?

When I went back to live with my mother she decided to move to a new town in New Jersey which happened to be the town that my biological father lived in. She moved across town, so I never really had any contact with him even though we lived in the same town. I never really understood why he did not want anything to do with me, but that is the way it worked out.

We moved into this big house and my mother had taken in a boarder who was nuts. She would wear pink slipper feet pajamas and she was in her thirties. That woman did not really last too long, and since my mother needed help with the rent, she invited another woman into the house whom she worked with. This woman would influence my life in ways I had not imagined at that time.

She was twenty-four and gorgeous, and she liked to party, after which she would come home smashed and flirt with me, even though I was just fourteen. Outside her room, there happened to be a small roof. So I would climb up the car port hop onto the small slanted roof, and look into her window. And as luck would have it, it was summertime, so she kept the window open. She liked to show off what she had, so she never closed the blinds.

So for the whole summer, she would come home smashed, and whatever happened while she'd been out determined how lucky I got. Sometimes she just went up to bed and didn't want to be bothered, but then there were the other times. She knew I always stayed up for her, so she would wait until I got on her roof, and then start to undress. Sometimes she would even put on music and strip, watching me watch her.

One night, during such a display, I happened to make a noise, and she pretended to be surprised at catching me and told me to "Get inside now!" But as I started to climb off the roof, she opened her screen and motioned for me to come in her room. That was the night I became a man by society's standards. For the next few months I was her boy toy, her plaything, but she taught me everything I needed to know to entice and tempt a women.

She and I had some good times together, and she taught me things I will never forget. At the end of that summer, she took me down to a place on the shore for a week and all we did was party. I was fourteen and free, with no rules, no time limits, and no problems. I met some of her friends, met some friends of my own, and had the time of my life. Looking back on it now, I think that that week was probably one of the most wonderful times of my life. But, though I did not know it then, it was to be my going away party.

As soon as I got back, my mother learned that she could sign a charge of incorrigibility, or delinquency, against me and the police would come and take me away. I did not spend another two weeks in her home again. Where I did spend my time, honestly—in fact, where I spent the rest of my growing-up years until almost age nineteen—was either in jail or on the streets.

It didn't take long to learn that there were two types of jail. One type was better than the other, but both were jail. One had no bars, and you could leave, the other had bars, and you could not leave.

It also didn't take long to learn that there is an unspoken code of conduct that exists both in jail and on the streets and that if you don't live by it, you can end up seriously hurt if not dead. In one form or another, the foundation principles (which I talk about more in Chapter 4) are present even in these shady places, and maybe even more so, because, on the streets or in jail, if you make one mistake, there are dire consequences. You see, these places take away everything you have, leaving you with nothing. In the end, all that's left are dignity, respect, honor, and integrity.

The first place I went to, called a JINS (Juveniles in Need of Supervision) facility, had numerous types of kids, but no bars and no armed guards. Instead, they had counselors. I was terrified the first time I went. I did not know what to expect.

I was just shy of fourteen, walking down the street and minding my own business, when a cop car pulled up to me. It was my dad. My mother had called him, knowing that he was a policeman in town. He got out of the car, told me I was under arrest for being incorrigible, and preceded to take me to the police department where he told all of the other officers that I was his son and that if they ever saw me, they should arrest me as I was probably up to no good. He embarrassed me and put me down, and that was the last time I really saw him except for another arrest or two throughout the years.

I had never had any kind of relationship with my dad. The only contact we'd had before that point was at Christmastime, and even that was not consistent from year to year. There was also a few weeks during the summer once or twice, but again, nothing consistent or lengthy.

At the time of my arrest, he was married with six kids of his own. His wife had once asked me if I would like to come live with them, but I had made the mistake of telling my mother about it. All contact with them stopped after that. I never remember him telling me he loved me, and I never remember him asking any questions about me, or taking any interest in my life at all.

Upon my first arrest, I was put into the system. And after my court appearance, I returned to the facility, as my mother refused to take me back. The facility became my home, and the people there became my family. My mother rarely came to see me, and whenever she did, there was a fight. I would always ask to come home and she would always refuse. It took a couple of months of this until I realized that I was not going back home.

It then occurred to me that I could just run away from the facility, and so I did. I started going to the Willow brook Mall, where the people I knew hung out. Then, like them, I did drugs and drank and basically became a hippy. I started listening to the Grateful Dead, and going to their concerts. I also listened to hard rock and southern rock.It was at that point that music became a big part of my life, and it remains so even to this day. Nights, I slept where I could—in backyards, garages, woods, people's homes, basements, cars, tents, you name it. I was truly "on the streets."

Every so often, I was rearrested, but all they could do was put me back into JINS, because I never committed any crimes. From there, I'd run away and the cycle would start all over again. At some point, because I had run away so often, they placed me in the juvenile detention center with bars, where there was no coming and going. Juvenile detention was lock-up. People went there because they had committed crimes. And so, naturally, this is where I learned to be a criminal.

Don't get me wrong—I was no angle. I had gotten high, run away from home, and even shoplifted a few times. But I was in no way a criminal. This all changed in detention. I went from being an innocent kid pretending to be tough, to a kid who truly knew what it meant to be tough. Having to fight for my right to stay straight, defend myself from aggressors, stay constantly on the alert, and try not to talk too much, all just to make sure I didn't end up dead or seriously hurt.

I got to know the rules of the road, so to speak, and I learned that there are two types of people in jail: those who get picked on and those who do the picking. If you show any vulnerability whatsoever, you are considered weak, and your fate is decided for you. Staying tough, keeping to your "own kind," and staying ahead of others is the key to survival. There are factions and gangs, and a lot of racial segregation, and there were often fights among these various groups. Fighting, in fact, was a way of life. You learned to sleep with your back to the wall and to sleep light, always ready for whatever might come. Because I spent the majority of my adolescent years in one lock-up or another, I learned to adapt quickly. I was able to rise up the ranks of the hierarchy, becoming well-known among the criminal community.

This sort of life, especially if you live it for any length of time, changes you forever. Certain things die in you, and the only way to become normal again is to have God do a work in your life. That said, I remember one particular incident in jail that broke something inside me and changed me forever, but it had nothing to do with the inmates. While in the JINS facility, my mother came and, with permission from the court, took out a girl, but left me there. I was not the same after witnessing that. I became very hard, uncaring, and vindictive. I taught myself to hate and to distrust everything. I cut off my emotions.

11

I fed on resentment. Everything that was supposed to have happened to an adolescent did not happen to me. I never went to high school. I never went to a prom. I never graduated. I never had a home. I had lost my innocence, and I suspected everyone of trying to get over on me. Distrust became my usual state. I was definitely not normal, and I felt I had missed out on life. I felt cheated.

Three: **But God**

I can remember sitting in a cell at fourteen or so, thinking that when I grew up, if I survived that long, I wanted to help others like me, so that another kid who was unwanted would have a place to go, or at least someone who understood. I wanted to do this because there were a few counselors that, if not for them, I may not be here. They were responsible for keeping me somewhat human, from never crossing that line that would have made me an animal.

You see, there is a point that people can cross which allows them to do horrible things and not care. It's like a mental breaking point that, once crossed, is almost impossible to come back from. The only way back is by an act of Jesus Christ. Luckily, those few who cared about me were able to keep me from that place of no return, by helping me remember my human side. I can never thank them. I wish I knew where they were so I could express my appreciation and let them see what God has done, but I am not even sure they are all still alive.

One of the most influential experiences in my life happened during this time. I was in the JINS facility and was hoping to still try to get home but it was not to be, but my mother had met a girl at the center on one of the few occasions she actually visited me. She actually went to court, and got her released to her, they became roommates for the next ten or twelve years. I was left to the system, and not allowed to go home. After that I did not want to get released to my mother. That was the time that something in me died towards her, and it has never come back. You just do not do something like that, I was never able to understand that action.

My trips back and forth between JINS and detention finally stopped one year, when I ran off to Florida. I met a kid at the J.I.N.S. facility that stated that he had people in Florida, and that if I ever got out that they would be able to put me up, so the next time I ran, I went to his house. His parents put me up for a while, just until they got me a bus ticket and off I went. When I got down to Florida, the people whose home I was going to were never told about me coming, they found out on the phone as I was standing in front of them. Needles to say, it did not make for a wonderful time. I was to stay at their house for the next six months. I tried to find work, but being an adolescent, a runaway, and wanted, the job market is limited. I found a girlfriend down there, got into partying and involved in all the stuff I was running away from.

I lasted about six or so months before I got turned in one afternoon. The guy I was staying with had decided that he liked the girl I was with, so he called the police and they came and got me. It was all over a girl. I was placed in a center for adolescents with no charges, and got flown back to New Jersey. I was placed in detention because I'd just run away too many times. They were not taking any chances any more. It was the judges orders that the system find me someplace to go as it was obvious that I was not going to go home and the centers were not working out as they were not meant for long term housing. So, after some testing it was decided to place me in a residential school.

After that, I was placed in the Bonnie Brae Residential School for eighteen months, where they tried to teach me right from wrong. They had teachers and you lived in what they called cottages with about a dozen other kids. There were no bars or armed guards, but it was known that you could not leave.

We had to graduate through the cottages to get released. I spent just shy of two years there, during which time I worked my way through the cottages and got away with just about everything. I was able to hang with other kids and get an education, although I really did not learn anything. I figured it was just somewhere they could put me to kill time. Of course, it didn't help that I was also getting high the whole time.

While there, I did get more of an education. About three quarters of the program through me and this other guy there got the idea to go visit a girl I knew from my dead head days. We called and she states to us to come on down, as she lived in GA.. So, we took a truck that was used for farm purposes and just left. We actually made it all the way down to West VA. Before we got caught. We were dropping off a hitchhiker off at their home and were waiting for gas money and food when we noticed that he was not coming back out, so we left, but before we could get back on the highway we were stopped for having a tail light out. Of course we lied, but they found out who we were, and all hell broke loose. More cops showed up, guns got drawn, and we were in deep crap.

We were arrested on eight or ten federal charges, and twenty six or so state charges, bail was set, and we were locked up. We were placed with juviniles, or at least I was. I found out later that he took all the charges on himself, I was actually never charged with anything. He had stated that he took the truck, stole the money he had on him, and forced me to go with his as I saw him leave. The authorities bought this story, and I was returned back to the detention center to await extradition back to New Jersey. I was flown into Newark Airport and returned to detention center to await return to the residential school.

I was able to return to Bonnie Bray Residential School and finish out their program, this is where I met two of the counselors that I now feel was instrumental in saving my life. I do not remember their names, but I remember that they were a male and female role model for me, they cared and that meant a lot. I also met some other kids there that remained friends for a while, but ultimately, as with the rest of my young life, nothing from it lasted.

After graduating from the residential school, I went to live with my uncle in New Hampshire. I was still very immature, though, and not willing to grow up, so I did not make it there long. While he was into making me responsible for me, I was into partying, getting over, and staying as irresponsible as possible. So, of course, there was no meeting of the minds, and we were in constant opposition with each other. At the time, I thought nothing about it, but now, looking back, I wish I had taken advantage of opportunity he gave me to grow as a person. He really went out of his way to set me up for a successful future; I was just too stupid to see it at the time. He got me a job, set me up in his house, and left me mostly alone, and I abused it. So, in less than six months he called my mother and he sent me back to New Jersey. Of course, this started the whole process over again.

By this point, I was doing drugs all the time, sleeping with any girl I could, and just looking out for number one. I had killed all my emotions by then and cut myself off from anything internal that could be considered weak. I followed the code of conduct: never let yourself be exposed, and always cover your butt. All things in life came down to manipulation, conning, cheating, lying, and getting over. I truly believe there was nothing good or honest in me during this time. I was just a hard, nasty, hateful individual. Still, there was always that little part of me, way down underneath, that hurt. It was that still-human part of me that kept me from killing anyone. Even as bad as I got, I could have never brought myself to do that.

After returning to New Jersey, I fell in with a gang called the Black Widows. They were from West Patterson, and they were interested in hanging with my group called the War Lords. The War Lords gang started when a bunch of us kids—all delinquents—banded together, and hung out at the mall's Fun and Games arcade. The War Lords found a home there, as we protected the arcade in return for the owner taking us to dinner, giving us free run of the place, and basically making sure we had what we needed to get by. It was a good arrangement, and I worked my way up to sergeant of arms, and then ultimately to president.

You see, in gangs, there is a chain of command that is followed and enforced strictly. This goes back to the idea that the underbelly of society is also built upon principles; it's just that those principles are handled in a very different way. The saying that there is honor among thieves is true, at some level anyway. In fact, it is why gangs are created and why they survive. On the streets and in jail, as you quickly learn that survival is for only the fittest, you learn that to be among the "fittest," you have to be a part of something bigger than yourself.

My time with the War Lords lasted until I was seventeen and arrested for the last time as a juvenile. When I went to prison, I lost track of them, as they had no presence in prison, and when I got out, they were no more.

I was a very angry individual and was into doing break ins and whatever else I had to; just to get money. I was living on the streets again as staying at my mother's home was not possible. I did come up with the bright idea to rob their home. I figured what the heck, if they could shut me out of their lives, I could steal from them as if they were no one special, so I did. I only got a few hundred dollars, nothing good, but it was enough for them to call the cops, press charges, and set me up to get caught.

As I was soon to find out, my mother and her friend knew the money was missing, but they could not prove it was me. So the friend got a hold of me and told me that she needed money for the holidays and that she knew of a house in West Milford, New Jersey, where she'd grown up, where we could score big. Unfortunately for me, I was under the influence and believed her, only to find out that it was a setup.

When we got there, the friend told me that she would stay in the car, as someone needed to watch, so I went in the house alone, with several stolen items on me—not just from my mom's but from other homes. I had been hanging out with people who were doing B&E's (breaking and entering with theft), and over a period of about six months, we had gotten good at it. At times we were doing three or four daily, so income was getting large. We had a fence set up where people would come and buy all of our stolen items for pretty good prices, so as sixteen- and seventeen-year-old kids, we were making a few hundred daily.

Little did I know, the cops were waiting for me outside the back door, their guns drawn in case I did something stupid. I went to jail, this time charged with a serious crime. I was in deep. So, here I am, seventeen, sitting in a jail, with no shoes or jacket (the police had taken them for evidence and never given them back). I was facing trial in court and serious jail time, and all because I had been set up by my mother and her girlfriend. Of course I know that the lifestyle was wrong and that I was living on borrowed time. I can't even tell you how many times that Jesus must have stepped in and saved me. We were in people's homes, we could have been shot at and killed. I was bound to get caught sooner or later, but at that point no one ever knew I was doing those things. There was no one to care, I was truly alone. I had no one who cared about me, no one who would have noticed if I had been shot. The friends I had were not real, they had no investment in my life, if I was with them, cool, if not no one noticed if I was there or not. Not even the gang I was in was that much different as when I went to jail, no one came, no one visited, no one ever let me know anything was ever going on again.

I was given a public defender—though the state defending you against the state never made any sense to me—and once all was said and done, I got a sentence of six years; two three-year sentences to be served back to back, instead of at the same time. It was the worst sentence you could get. It was one of the lowest times in my life.

I went to Yardville State Prison, then to Annandale State Prison, and finally after going in front of the classification board, served thirteen months in Stokes State Forest, which is an honor camp of the Annandale State Prison. The final sentence was given by the classification board, negating the sentence from the judge, which was legal in New Jersey. Once released, I was placed on state parole for five years, of which I served three with no trouble, and then I was off and free. My parole officer allowed me to do whatever I wanted and report every few weeks. As long as there was no trouble, I was free to go and do pretty much whatever I wanted. I got away with everything.

It was during this time, one night right before Christmas, that I met my wife. In a bar in Willow Brook Mall, I ran into a guy I had spent time with at Bonnie Brae, and she was with him. He invited me to join them, after which the three of us, along with my future wife's best friend, spent the night getting wasted. I ended up with the friend, and we parted after a night of debauchery. I did not see her again until six months later, when we met in a Seven-Eleven parking lot. I was heading for New York to cop drugs, and she was looking for a good time. We just fit each other, and for the next month or so, were constantly together, until I asked her to go steady. That was on July 4, and we have been together ever since. Of course we have had our ups and downs. For a few years in a row, we split up each summer, but ultimately our lives came into synch, and we are still together today. In fact on March 30, 2010, we celebrated twenty-five years of marriage.

We were both on drugs at the time, she in the minor league and I in the majors. We had our music in common, and her friends became my friends. I lived in the same town as she did now. I rented a room in a rooming house. I held many jobs, unable to keep any of them for an extended period due to my drugging and drinking. In fact, it would be more accurate to say that my *job* was dealing and taking drugs; working was just something I felt I had to do.

I was living in and out of several places, but with little money, and little care about myself, I was unstable, so I never really stayed any one place for long. Buy my wife was different, as was her family. I had digressed to the point where I was sleeping behind her garage and in her room when she could sneak me in, so things were desperate. One morning I got caught by her father in the garage, and he was not really fond of me so he was yelling at me to get off his property, and stated to me "Don't you have a home to go to?" and when I stated to him that I did not, he just shook his head, got his wife and walked away. His wife got me breakfast, got me cleaned up, and allowed me to start to stay inside.

They gave me a place to get my life together, and a shower on a regular basis. Hot water, heat, warmth, comfort, these were things that were foreign to me at that time of my life. But, I was young; I had survived that way forever. It was usual for me to not eat for days at a time, to take showers in truck stops. To sleep in tents, alleys, basements, and in cars was common for me. I was officially homeless for most of my juvenile years.

Our core group of friends consisted of about eight or ten of us who were together almost all the time. We hung out in Caldwell where we lived, every night, going to concerts, doing drugs, hopping the bars, and just basically being bums. Some of the group was homeless, but the others would always help accommodate them. We were all coming of age, seeking what it meant to be grown-up, and wondering what life had in store. We lived this life for about three years, until finally, my wife and I married, and soon after our son was born.

We figured we needed to stop doing things. We wanted to change our lives, and we needed to get things going. We decided that a child was what would allow us to do this. As I am sure most of you know, it did not help, it got worse after my son was born as I could not seem to quite partying. Her brothers were all carpet layers, flooring installers, so I was taught a trade. I was able to get the basics of flooring, and it started to come easy to me and I got good at it. I ended up becoming an installer for the next twenty five years.

My wife was able to just quit partying. I, on the other hand, was neither able nor willing to stop. My life revolved around partying. Everything I knew centered on doing drugs, which, for me, consisted mostly of large amounts of cocaine and alcohol. I could never get my crap together long enough to keep sober, and I spent all our money partying. I would use up my entire paycheck within hours of getting it.

This kept on throughout the next six years, through the birth of all our children. So unfortunately, each one of them was born into my addiction. Luckily, my wife was able to stay sober and clean the entire time, but this was a very hard time for her and the children. I was not to get clean, for good, for another six years. During this time my wife had taken to talking to my mother. My mother had heard of a missionary training school about ten or so hours away from where she was, and she stated to my wife that it might be just the place for me to get clean and sober. So, we were able to sell everything, and we took the two children, and one on the way and sold everything and moved to Az.

The missionary training center was called the "The Ranch". The camp was run by a woman who claimed to be a prophet of God, which we were desperate enough to believe at that point. So I moved to California and stayed at "The Ranch". My mother had been teaching in a town in New Jersey, but had decided that God called her to Az to help those on the

Navajo Reservation. So, she just up and left her job of many years and went. My wife and children went to live with her for the first few months of my training.

After six months of living this way, my wife and kids moved in with me at the Ranch, as my mother's place was too cramped for all of them. However, that did not last long either, as my wife decided that the Ranch was a cult, and too far out for her. She finally told me that it was either her or the Ranch. Of course, she won, so we moved. As luck would have it, about five miles from where my mother taught on the Navajo reservation, a Navajo chieftain's family wanted the help of missionaries to get a TV complex up and running on their retreat. So we stayed on the retreat and helped them in exchange for living means. In addition to the TV complex, the family retreat had a school and an orphanage.

We stayed there just long enough for me to get involved with a Christian television center in California that provided the complex with a television replicator, a few cameras, and a transceiver, which we used to relay programming from a Christian station when not airing original productions. (We filmed, for example, the dedication of the new station, the government's acceptance of a new Christian television station, and the subsequent handing over of the station's management to the Navajo Nation.) As we finished the process of training, requisitioning materials, and gaining funds, the family told us that we would either have to leave or support ourselves. We had no one to sponsor us, so we were on our own. The whole thing took about nine months, in which time I was able to stay sober. But it was not to last.

We moved to Page, Arizona. Page Az offered the closest city from where my mother lived. My wife had just had another baby, so we wanted to be in a city, and she wanted to be within reach of my mother for support with a new born. We went to the local penacostal church. I found various jobs thereafter, and of course found the people who partied. It was not long before I was, once again, drinking and doing drugs with a vengeance, and was thereafter rejected by the local church. We went back on public assistance, living poorly again, until we had an opportunity to move back to the Northeast. My wife's sister had just lost her husband to drunk driving, and she was raising three small children by herself, so it seemed like the perfect situation—she would have help, my wife would have help, and we would have a place to live, and everything would be wonderful again.

Unfortunately, we had left one thing out of the equation: me. We made it back without any issues, and lasted about six weeks, until I started working in Jersey again, at which point I stopped in a bar on the way home and got so drunk that I blacked out. When I came to, I decided to drive anyway, and using my wife's sister's pickup, pulled into oncoming traffic. I was hit by (as luck would have it) another drunk, who happened to be an important person in that county, and who happened to have a fiancée who happened to be the arresting officer. She never got into any trouble. I, on the other hand, was taken straight the Morris County Jail and given one call, to which my wife's answer was to hang up.

I spent only the weekend in jail, which I thought was weird, as others I had talked to were waiting six to nine months to get in front of the judge for a DUI. Looking back, however, I see that it directly contributed to my getting sober. I truly believe that if not for the events that occurred to me at this point in my life, I would not be here today. I was transported to the West Orange Township Jail and put in an eight-by-six cell for eight days. No change of clothes, no access to a shower, no ability to smoke—nothing but three meals a day, which I refused. I drank the coffee and sodas, but left the food.

I did pray. I prayed for the whole eight days. I asked God to get me out of the trouble I was in and promised him that for such relief, I would go straight. I was able to talk to my children once, at which point my wife told me that we would not be getting back together. She said that things had just gone too far, and that there was no going back. She said there was too much hurt, too much water under the bridge. She stated to me that it would take a miracle for us to get back together. Hearing this was hurtful and made me feel hopeless. I was looking at doing at least a hundred and ninety days in the county for my two DUIs, and that would include a ten-year loss of license and a nine thousand dollar fine. So after at least six months in jail, I would have nowhere to go, and I would have no money, no family, no clothes, no nothing.

So, I prayed. And the end of the eight days, I was walking into the courtroom when they said it was getting too late and the judge had to go. So I was put back in my cell until the night court adjourned. This time, just as I was going into the courtroom, the power failed. The backup power came on, but it did not include the computers, so, I was charged as if the DUI were my first instead of my third, and, to complete the miracle, I was let go. They processed me as a first-time offender, put me through probation, and I was back on the street in less than an hour. The power went back on as I left the court. I still believe it was a miracle of God. He placed me in a position in which I had to keep my word, which I did. I had told God that if he got me out of this trouble, that I would not party again. That was on June 14, 1990. I have not partied since.

I called my wife, who could not believe that I had been released and she told me that I could come back; but that she was not going to come and get me. I hitched home, which took me eight hours. Of course, the first person who picked me up was drinking and smoking a joint, but I refused it as I had made my bed, and I was going to lie in it. Immediately after making it home, I looked for a rehab center that would take me, even though I had no money and no insurance. It took a few weeks, but I finally found a place called the White House in Lake Areal, Pennsylvania, and I sat on their porch for two days until they took me in.

I stayed in for the entire twenty-eight days, and I learned what it took to get and stay sober. They gave me not only an education, but a way of life that allowed me to do what I had to, to get clean. Part of that lifestyle was the AA program, which I was involved in for the next ten-and-a-half years. To this day, I still say that God led me to AA, and that AA led me back to God.

Before, due to the abuse that I had received as a child in the name of religion, I was so hardened against God that I did not even want to hear his name mentioned. If the subject was brought up too much, I would get violent and leave the room. Yet even back then, I could get that a power greater than I was in charge, and that is what ultimately led to my understanding of the difference between a relationship with God and religion during my rehab years. (I will get into this difference later in this book.) Suffice it to say, however, I learned quite a lot about what God had in mind for me in the ensuing years.

Unfortunately, the second year of my sobriety, I had a nail go through my wrist at work, and it took four more years and four surgeries to get to a point where I would not only not lose my hand, but also be able to use some of it. There was a lot of opposition to my being on pain medication, but the difference between me and others was that I always talked about the pain, as well as the medication. In the end, I stayed sober, and to me that was what mattered. There are many different schools of thought about people and recovery and pain medication. I was not a super hero; I was not going to tuff it out to keep others happy. I knew there was a lot of pain. I knew if I spoke about it, kept others appraised of what was going on in my life, and there were no secrets, it would be ok, and it was.

During this time, I continued following the Grateful Dead, going on tour for a few weeks each year, but staying clean. I stayed sober for ten-and-a-half years.

Then, on our fifteenth anniversary, I bought five dozen roses and took my wife to a fancy restaurant where we drank champagne. From that point on, I resumed my drinking, except that it never progressed to an unhealthy habit. I drink to this day with no issues at all. I believe it is because God delivered me from the disease.

I was also privileged enough to go back to school in 1995 and earn a bachelor's degree in Human Services from Scranton University. I did the four-year degree program in three and a half; not too shabby for a kid who never went past sixth grade, and earned his high school degree in prison. I had a minor in religion and one in philosophy.

I then started the graduate program at Scranton, which should have taken about three to four years part-time, had I not been hit by a drunk driver in 2001, which totally changed my life. I had to take a few years off from school because, altogether, between my wrist and my neck, I went through six major operations. Unfortunately, they were not fully successful, so I remain a chronic-pain patient to this day. I did finally earn my graduate degree in 2006, however, after which I sat for state certification. After that, My wife and I started a corporation called Alpha & Omega Counseling Center to help people who need counseling who cannot afford it to get it. I volunteer when I am able, and my wife does the books. We do the best we can with what we have. Being a chronic-pain patient took me to places that I never thought I would go. There is a whole world out there that many do not know exists. This world, filled with doctors, insurance companies, and attorneys, can be very dark, not only in terms of navigating the system to get the help you need, but also in regard to risking necessary prescription-drug dependency, which may include bouts of withdrawal. If you or someone you know is a chronic-pain patient, you will want to read the Afterword at the end of this book, which talks more about living in such a world.

Suffice it to say here, there was a brief time in my life that I was on Oxycontin, which is a highly addictive prescription drug. It almost drove me to do things that I would have never done at any other time, and it sent me to places that I had once sworn I would never go back to.

What I learned is that once you take an opiate-based pain medication, your body becomes dependent on it to the point that you must take it at regular intervals, whether you are feeling pain or not. When you are feeling pain chronically, however, your mind tends to play a terrible trick on you, telling you that if one dose works well, then two will work better, and three will really do the trick, and so forth and so on. As a result, I found a doctor out on Long Island who would prescribe the medication for me in addition to my regular doctor, so I ended up taking twice the medication I should have. Every two weeks, I found myself driving four hours each way just to get a second prescription. This lasted about eight or nine months, until, by the grace of God, I was sent to another doctor who switched me to a less addictive drug called MS Contin, at which point the addiction issues went away literally overnight.

Through all of this, in August 2004, I gave my life back to Christ, and since then, I have changed drastically. So many things have changed since that day that it would take the rest of this book to tell you everything, but I would like to take some time to talk about three main perspectives that I have gained since then. One, I am saved by grace. Two, no act I can do will ever be good enough, so I need to rely on the grace of God for everything. And three, performance-based Christianity does not work; we were called by Jesus in our sin, before we were even able to clean ourselves up, which says that Jesus is not afraid to get dirty. He loves us wherever we are, and he knows what he is getting—we are no surprise to him. He knew us before time, space, and creation. Before understanding these three ideas, I thought that being a Christian was all performance-based, because that was what I had been taught growing up. I just did not know any better.

Now, I see that change is possible to the extent that I allow Christ to work in my life. As such, Christ has to be the center of all I do. First, I had to allow Christ into my life, and then let him live in my life, and now I have to keep him at the center, which takes work; *walking* with Jesus is a verb.

Today, life *is*. There are ups and downs. I live life today, while learning to seek God and his will for my life, and to just *be* in Christ. And whenever something goes wrong, whenever things seem to be falling apart, or whenever I feel like I have just not heard from God in awhile, I have to remember that feelings are just that—feelings. They are not real, they cannot be counted on, and given time, they will change.

In all things, regardless of what *is* right now, I have to think, "but God … " In other words, yes, life may feel miserable in the moment, but then there's God. And with God, all things are possible. So we must continue to keep him at the center and to live our lives as he wants us to, so that we can bear good fruit. Even in the middle of some of the horrible things we have to go through, if we keep our eyes on Christ, we can have a breakthrough with him.

If you get nothing else from my story, I hope that you get this: all hope is not lost. Just remember, "but God … "

Four: **The Foundation Principles at Home**

Throughout my life, I have found seven principles to be the foundation of all morals, they are dignity, honor, respect, integrity, mercy, grace, and unmerited favor. These seven principles must be present in each of our lives in order for us to be complete. These principles are at the very core of our existence. If we want to be the best we can be, and if we profess to live a Godly life, these principles must be active in us. In fact, they must be the foundation that our lives are built upon. These seven principles can be found throughout all great pieces of literature, all great men and women, and every great society.

These principles have, at their core, the ability to bring a person to greatness, to help them achieve at heights that they had never expected to. They are responsible for all the great decisions ever made, whether in the underbelly of society or in the elite of society. America was based upon them for its first one hundred fifty years, although for many years now they have been bred out of our culture by decimating the family, attempting to remove God from everything, and trying to replace the family unit with government. The result is the out-of-control society we live in today.

The family is the first place many of us are introduced to values. If we see our guardians using these seven principles to guide them in every step and every major decision, we come to trust, as we grow into maturity, that if we also work with these values, we too will accomplish the things they did. We learn that if we act with these seven principles in our hearts and minds—dignity, honor, respect, integrity, mercy, grace, and unmerited favor—keeping God first in our lives, that we will be able to have more than our parents had. Our kids, by using these techniques, will have more than we have, and so it goes through the generations. On the other hand, if we grow up seeing our guardians practice hatred, bigotry, prejudice, and bias, we will grow up feeling discontentedness, hatred, anger, frustration, and a sense of entitlement.

Either way, we take in what we see happening around us as we grow. Watching and copying the behavior of our guardians in this way is called modeling. We see their behaviors, their likes, their dislikes, and their beliefs. We come to understand what they consider valuable and what they see as normal, and we consider these things normal and valuable, as well. So, how our parents behave, what they believe in, and what views they hold will determine our own beliefs, viewpoints, and behaviors, either for the positive or negative. We take on their ideals, morals, and mores, for better or for worse.

In my home, I did not see the foundation principles at work. Instead, I witnessed violence and many forms of brutality; the emotional type, I think, is the worst, but there is also physical, spiritual, sexual, and mental brutality. These forms are all equally devastating to the young person, as you grow up always wondering what you did wrong or whether your are really that bad. As those feelings grow, there is a point when you start to develop ways of escaping from them rather than dealing with them, as what is going on is just too great to deal with. You learn to watch for signs, to detect certain attitudes, and then to become invisible. And finally, if you get caught doing something that you shouldn't in order to escape, you learn how to go away to a place where no one can hurt you.

This view does not take into account the gang lifestyle. There are certain advantages to being in a gang, especially when you live in a place where, to survive, you have to join one. In some cities, where you are considered old by the time you hit thirty, especially among the lower economic classes, joining gangs becomes an accepted way of life. For those kids who live in such a place, there is very little choice. And once initiated into a gang, one usually never gets out. Membership is for life.

Also, to get into a gang, taking a life is often required, and, since today we place so little value on life, it is not uncommon for the pledging member to be eager to show his or her courage.

Five: **The Fall of Society and Family**

Our society was formed on the premise that we would be free to gather wherever we wanted, pray to whatever god we wanted, and associate with whoever we wanted. Basically, we were free to do whatever we wanted as long as it would not hurt another.

If you look back at the forties, fifties, and early sixties, a sense of innocence seemed to permeate society as a whole. We were a nation that put God first. We placed great emphasis on God, church, and the Sabbath (including blue laws that allowed us not to work on Sundays).

We looked out for one another then, too. We were close with our families, we took pride in our neighborhoods, and we knew what the rules were. Oh, you knew what you could get away with and how far you could push, but there was a sense of decency in everything. A clear line was evident, and you did not dare go past it; you knew that certain things were just unacceptable. There was discipline and there were consequences for actions, including spankings, not only by parents but by teachers as well. This was all common, accepted, and the norm.

Unfortunately, we as a society have descended from that point. Modern life principles seem to include "A little white lie does no harm" and "It's not how you play the game; it's whether you win or lose." You've also heard, "If it feels good, do it" or, even, "If someone else has it, take it. Everyone will understand; it's survival of the fittest." And once someone is able to justify taking another's life, identity, property, money, spouse, or children, covetousness becomes a commonplace ideal and society is headed for a rude awakening.

We want instant results. We tap our foot in front of the microwave, so to speak. We also, as a whole, seem to feel that we are entitled. We think that every time we want something, we should get it—and, as a result, we have lost the incentive for work. In my opinion, this is one of the biggest issues that our society faces at the present time; we have forgotten to look to the past and see that hard work is what made our country great.

And all of this degraded morality has fostered a sense of paranoia. Life has no value; because of what we call free will, we feel entitled to treat our children and families and everyone else like garbage; we have become desensitized to violence because we watch it every day on TV; no place seems safe because people are attacked in schools, churches, malls, and homes, leaving no place sacred. Thus everyone is sure that everyone else is out to get them, and we break down into a society of people who have no sense of security and who distrust everyone and everything.

As a result, society has gone from one that left its doors open at night many years ago, to a society that not only locks up, but has more and more people carrying guns every day. We have gone from having a culture in which neighbors not only associated with, but also got to know, one another, to having one in which we do not even know the people next door, let alone those down the street.

This is not to say that there were not things that were wrong back in the day. We all know that things are never perfect. There have always been people who do horrible things. There have always been parents who are abusive and neglectful. There have always been those who hurt others for fun. But *as a whole,* we as a society were more Bible-based, more caring, and more trusting then; we took care not to offend, we attended church in greater numbers, and we generally felt the government was looking out for us.

It was in the early sixties when society changed as a whole. Ideas were challenged and we changed our perception of things. Laws were altered, and along with them, people and social norms. A whole generation was hardened as what was acceptable became more brazen. Things that were before done behind closed doors, because they were considered wrong, were now done in the public eye and, for the most part, accepted. Free love, sex, drugs, and rock and roll was the battle cry of the next three decades.

Prayer was taken out of schools, and the government got into a war that unnecessarily killed our kids. Families started to suffer, as dads were leaving and not coming back, making one-parent families almost the norm. As violence, hatred, and polarized economic situations were broadcast everywhere, television became king. We could now see horrible things happening as they happened. And with that advent, we became a global community.

Then, with the decline of the family, the loss of the two-parent home, and the loss of God as the rule, the breakdown of society sped up. Even at the local level, we replaced God with government. We took power away from the family and gave it to schools and agencies, by outlawing corporal punishment and then instructing kids to tell teachers or government officials if they got "hit" at home. In turn, parents were charged with crimes for punishing their kids. In essence, by doing this, we only undermined confidence in the family, sending kids the message that they should, instead, trust schools and government agencies, thus cutting the family off at the knees. At the same time, we gave up church as a foundation, turning from God and putting our trust into capitalism, the government, and media.

Unfortunately, we took a system that worked very well, and we destroyed it. But then we could not fathom why society seemed to be going to hell in a hand basket. And we could not understand why our children were no longer learning and practicing the foundation principles.

Now, nothing in itself is bad. Everything in balance is acceptable. The problem is not the media, the school, or the government. The issue is that we have become unbalanced in our thinking and living. We went from reliance on a well-balanced diet of God, country, and freedom, to dependence on our government alone to decide what we *should* think of as right or acceptable. In short, we have gone from a nation of people who knew what was right to one that had to be told what was right.

As a result, we have become a people who no longer want to get involved. We fear being sued or charged with some criminal act for being "intrusive." This is especially sad because for many kids, home is still the problem. And let me tell you, when you are scared to go home because you never know what is waiting for you, it is bad enough. But with others not wanting to get involved, home becomes a dungeon, and no one knows the horror that occurs there. Because no one wants to get sued, no one comes to your door when they hear the screams to put a stop to the violence. Thus, the violence perpetuates itself. Kids grow up thinking that this way of life is normal, that, instead of abuse, they are receiving discipline, and thus it goes from one generation to another.

Six: **The Answer**

The men and women who built our country did so based on the principles of the Bible. The founding fathers included scripture in original drafts of the Declaration of Independence, as well as in other writings we hold to be true and sacred today, such as the Gettysburg Address, and the Constatution that we live by, yet those quotes from the Bible are now conspicuous in their absence. Worse, the history being taught today is not the history that was taught a hundred and fifty years ago. The history books are being changed to fit the morals and opinions of those in power, and again, with Bible references conspicuously missing.

How did this happen? Where are all the folks that profess to be the watchdogs of our society? The answer is not pretty. As the real watchdogs of our society are getting older, things are getting past them, and little to no relief is coming forward to take their place. You can not have people step up and take over if they are not being taught what it is that has gone on before them. Add to that the idea that to stand for something and not bend is not exactly fashionable today, and that right and wrong are widely accepted as relative ideas, and not absolutes (we are told there is no real black and white, but that everything is shaded in gray), and maybe you can begin to see the root of our problem.

But what, then, is the answer? It is found within the Word of God, and in what Jesus said is the most important commandment: "Love your neighbor as you love yourself, and love the Lord your God with all your heart, with all your might, and with all your soul."Matthew 22:37-40. (Your soul is your mind, your will, and your emotions.) The word of God promises us that if you do this, all will be well with you. These two commandments were added by Christ as he was speaking to his disciples before he was crucified, and they really sum up all of the other commandments. If followed, these commandments hold profound implications for our lives.

Love is a tricky word. We have, in the English language, only one definition for the word. Yet in Greek, there are four definitions, depending on how it is used. For example, in one sense of the word, *love* has deep-rooted meaning. It is that all-knowing, all-accepting, all-forgiving, all-encompassing kind of love spoken of in the Bible, the kind that Jesus had for us as he hung on the cross. Jesus said that there is nothing greater than this kind of love; that everything in life is based upon it. The Greek word for this kind of love is called agape (a-gah-pay). For the purposes of this book, agape is what is being referred to whenever love is mentioned. This is important to note, because in our society, the word is so overused that it has lost its original meaning. We love ice cream, for example, and we love movies and puppies.

The answer is to put love at the foundation of our lives and our society. As we all know, a foundation is imperative to keep a structure standing. If a foundation is solid, everything else on top of it can be fixed, but if a foundation is faulty, you can be fairly assured that the whole structure is unsafe. So, the important question to ask ourselves at this point is, "How is our foundation? Are we structurally sound?"

To answer this question on a personal level, you must look at how you were raised. Certain indicators, such as these, will quickly allow you to see whether you have a sound foundation:

- You are willing to take direction.
- You ask for help.
- You give of yourself without expecting anything in return.
- You react positively even when things do not go your way.

As stated earlier, and this is in accordance with all of the great child psychologists of our time, children will do what they see their parents doing. It is that simple concept called modeling. As you grow from an infant to a toddler, you start to take note of your surroundings. You notice people's attitudes, feelings, and emotions. You begin to get a sense of right and wrong, and mimic the behavior of the adults you interact with daily.

As a general rule, you learn what you see and not what you hear. A mother can tell you something is one way until she is blue in the face, but if her actions say otherwise, you will trust what you see being done over what you hear being said. When a guardian's words and actions do not lineup is when trouble arises for a child. The child will model what he sees the parent doing, but will then be punished for it. This conflicting messaging starts to undermine what the child understands as reality, and you begin to question the very fabric of your world. Such questioning and insecurity, as this child grows, spreads to every area of life, seriously affecting self-esteem, self-worth, and self-perception. In turn, a child's total belief system, faith base, and his relationships with himself and others are thrown off-base. We must have everything line up. What we say and what we do are very important as when things match up, we learn to trust what we hear, what we see, and what we know, thus we can have love for everything as we learn that everything is lining up with the word of God, thus we see it lived out before us.

The lack of a sound foundation in many homes then translates into that same lack in society. It is why we have the gang problem we have today, as well as the need for therapists, counselors, and psychologists. It is also the reason we are overly reliant, as a society, on medication such as antidepressants, mood elevators, and antipsychotics. At the root of all these issues is that we have lost the agape kind of love. We no longer value family and Christ as the center of all things.

Added to this problem is the fact that many of us, in regard to what we see as the norm, have allowed ourselves to be lulled into complacency by the authorities. Now, the normal home has only one parent and the normal school has metal detectors and guards patrolling the hallways. Gangs in our schools and kids killing kids have become a way of life. Disgruntled citizens shooting in places of business, retail establishments, and colleges have become commonplace. Even in the church, we have allowed ourselves to sleep through a divorce rate of over 55 percent. And we have allowed Christian prayer to be taken out of schools, town hall meetings, and public arenas, all while accepting the public expressions of other religions.

We have also allowed ourselves to be lulled into a false sense of security by spiritual "leaders" who are themselves asleep, with little to no relationship with the Holy Spirit. This is evidenced by the number of churches that have no idea that the power of the Holy Spirit is for today as much as it was for yesterday. And, we have allowed the exact thing that Paul warned about in his letters to the Galatians to not only happen but to become common practice: we have allowed the formation of denominations. "A house divided against itself cannot stand,"(Matthew 12:25) both Jesus and Paul said, and we can see that truth now; there is little power in the body of Christ, due to the body being split into factions.

A final factor adding to the problem is that we have become a society that relies on quick fixes. We bandage the broken part of ourselves instead of actually taking the time to fix it the right way—which is often from the ground up. We build upon a broken foundation, and the result is something that was skewed from the start. It is not possible to build a structure straight up on a foundation that is crooked.

The sad part of all this is that the starts out so small, so seemingly insignificant that you hardly notice the compromise. But as time goes forward, there is another compromise, and another, until what was once off-limits, not thinkable, unimaginable, becomes commonplace. If we are not careful, it is in this way that we may compromise ourselves right into hell.

We need to be a Christian community that starts in love. Ends in love, and has its existence in love. We cannot allow compromise to derail us from our primary purpose, which is to show the country that in Christ, love is the rule that we live by. That all things are possible through love, that we can love someone back from the brink of destruction. We can love people right back into the kingdom. We need to have our actions line up with our words, and have the actions and words line up with the word of God.

Seven: Personal Change

hallenges are placed in our life for a reason. They allow us to grow and mature. And they test how much we have learned from the past, allowing us to put into practice those fundamental lessons we have picked up along the way. In fact, when I face challenges, I find that they are usually trying me in an area in which Jesus has already been trying to teach me. You see, God knows that at those times when our lives are a mess, when everything we touch seems to turn to garbage, we are most able to reflect upon our personal history and see what we have made ourselves into. During such times, it is crucial that we be honest with ourselves. If we do not like what we see, we need to admit that we, in fact, do not know it all, and that there is still much left to learn.

Of course, our first reaction is not usually to take the blame ourselves. We want to point the finger. We may blame God, asking him questions like, "How could you do this to me?" or "Why did you let this happen, if you were watching out for me?" Although when we ask these questions, we are not really looking for the answers so much as we are looking to blame. We ask these questions to deflect the blame, instead of looking at ourselves and being willing to do what it takes to change. We fail to remember that God did not put us here; we put ourselves here by compromising somewhere along the line.

Or, if we're not too busy blaming God, we may blame the devil for everything that is wrong in our lives. We may also look to blame others around us. When we get ticketed for speeding because we're late for work, we blame the officer instead of ourselves for sleeping in. Or, when our kids get into trouble at school, we blame the school teacher, principle, or guidance counselor—after all, if they just kept the kids in line, there wouldn't be a problem. But in reality, it is our responsibility—not the school's—to make sure our kids do their homework and are getting help in any areas in which they might be struggling. We, not the school, are raising our kids. But when our children are in daycare from six months old until school age, or we look to afterschool activities to keep them busy while we work, or we leave them alone at home without supervision, we then cannot wonder why we have no relationship with them.

You see, we have this thing called free will. Free will allows us to do whatever we choose. We are the only ones living our life. We are the only ones making our choices. So, it would stand to reason that we are the only ones to blame when things go wrong. Yet we look everywhere but at ourselves. We have excuses lined up that we have used for ages, even though, in most cases, they are not valid. We will find any way possible to assuage the blame, so we don't have to face the harsh reality that our lives have become what they are because of us.

We need to take responsibility for our families and ourselves. It is the way of God to be responsible for what God has given us. Remember that although Jesus has a plan for your life, so does the enemy. There are a myriad of ways that the enemy can snag you and make you ineffective to God—and if he does, he wins. If you are too busy trying to do everything else but what God asked you to do, he wins. If you are so heavenly minded that you are no earthly good, he wins. If your faith is so toxic that no one else wants a part of it, he wins. If religion takes over your life, he wins. This is why Jesus stated in the gospels, "Broad is the path, straight and smooth, that leads to destruction, but small and narrow is the path that leads to the Kingdom of God."(Said another way, there are many paths to destruction, but only one that leads to Christ, and that path is through Jesus Christ, the son of God. He is the answer to all questions, the solution to all problems, and the key that unlocks eternal and abundant life.

He is also the one who imparts to us the seven principles: honor, dignity, respect, integrity, grace, mercy, and love. Without these seven, you are nothing. You alone choose whether to offer them up, both to yourself and to others, and no one can take them from you or force you to give them away. In other words, you alone decide how you treat others and yourself. Even if someone is treating you horribly, you choose how to treat them in return. This is why Jesus was able to tell us to turn the other cheek. Jesus knew that, through him, we could control ourselves. He knew that even in the worst of circumstances, we could still bring ourselves to offer up one of these seven principles, because all Godly things are possible through Christ.

Eight: Religion vs. Relationship

At this point, I think it is important to talk about the difference between religion and relationship. There are many different religions in the world today, not to mention many different denominations in just the Christian faith. So how are you supposed to know the right or true way to God?

The Bible states that there is only one way to salvation, and that is through Jesus Christ. You must totally believe that he is who the Bible says he is, and that through him all can be saved and everything made new. After all, the whole reason he came into the world was to make these truths known.

If you are struggling with your belief in the father or the son, here are a few things to think about. First, if you look back through the Old Testament, you can see that, time after time, prophets foretold his coming. There are also non-Jewish accounts of Jesus written by Josephus and other Roman historians who lived during the time of Christ. So, it is not just in the Bible that we find the name Jesus; it is in history as well.

Second, when you look around and notice how nature is put together—how the solar system is formed and how the human body is constructed—you should be able to see that we are not just random particles slapped together by chance. Of course, there are numerous debates over the validity of the theory of evolution, but consider that just as the creation theory takes faith, so does the evolution theory. Both are faith-based, because neither has evidence. There is no evidence of one species morphing into another. Are we capable of adapting to our environment? Of course. We can even adapt to severe climate and evolutionary catastrophes, if necessary—but these adaptations occur within a species.

So, for the purpose of this book, let us agree that we were created—brought out of nothing into something—by a supreme being. Let us believe that we were made originally from dust, to be in the image of the Most High, God himself, as it is written, "Let us make man in our image(Genesis 1:26)

But before we move on, let us also address the argument that, according to a literal translation of the Bible, we as a population are only six thousand years old. But the Bible also states that God's time is not like ours; time is not relative to him, as it is for us here on earth. In numerous places in the Bible, God states that "a thousand years is as a day, and a day is as a thousand years."(2 peter 3:8) God never states how old he is either. He says only that he is, has always has been, and always will be, so the concept of time is wasted on him.

We, however, do go by time in this dimension, so we have come up with ways to date things, and the ways man has measured our earth's time and history appears valid. Accepting that God's time is not man's, then, and vice versa, it is my opinion that carbon dating is fairly reliable, and that earth is older than six thousand years. However, this is one of those arguments that really means nothing; in fact, it is the epitome of the kind of argument that starts divisions within the Christian faith.

The first Christians were called "those of the way," because Christianity is a way of life. Religion is about head knowledge, but spirituality is about heart knowledge. Many of us have been hurt by religion. We have put up walls and cut off our hearts, so that we cannot be hurt again. But as a consequence, we have also lumped spirituality into the "religion" column as well, not knowing any better. It can take a long time for Christ to find another opening into your heart to affect change. Spirituality states that it is okay to test what's being said by the Word or by your pastor. It also says that it's okay to think for yourself and find a more personal path to walk with God.

But no matter how old the earth is, the Bible is still true. No matter what age we are living in, the Word of God is still the Word of God; thus, all that is in the Word of God is valid. If we believe part, then we need to believe all. The Bible was not written as a scientific book; it was written by inspiration of the Holy Spirit who related to us how God started things, how they progressed, and where they will end up Religion is man's way of controlling others. It's the idea that "you must go through the "us" to get to God; only we have the true way to heaven." Religion states that there must be specific, set ways of doing things, which, if not followed exactly, will result only in failure. Religion states that there must be uniformity, and that everyone must adhere to the same code of conduct or be ruined. Religion states that all other ways of doing things are evil. Religion states that there must be conformity—everyone must look and behave the same in order to have eternal life. And finally, religion states that one must go through its representatives to find the one true way to God.

A few more observations about religion: there appears to be a major focus on money and wealth; faith is based on fear, guilt, and shame (e.g., you are motivated to do right only for fear of stepping out of line); and force is often used to gain control of its members (e.g., more people have been murdered in the name of religion than in any other).

Relationship, on the other hand, is about a personal experience with Jesus. While religion is about control, relationship is about love. While religion is about having to do this or not doing that, relationship is about doing for another because you want to out of love.

Relationship is one on one. And with Christ, relationship is a personal investment of all you are, so that you can become all he wants; in other words, whatever we may sacrifice for relationship we get back tenfold in love, understanding, forgiveness, peace, hope, wisdom, and other fruits of the Spirit.

In the Bible, Christ states over and over again that he wants to have a relationship with his children. In numerous places, God states that the whole reason he sent his son was so that we could be in a relationship with him again. You see, sin separates us from God, but Jesus bridges that gap once and for all, so we can confidently ask him for whatever we want—and he will grant it as long as we are in his will.

His will. Now there is another trap set for springing. What truly is God's will for us, and how can we find it? God knows and has called each of us to something different in life, so his will may vary from person to person. But the beautiful thing about having a relationship with Jesus is that he will let you know his will through his word, and through your prayer and fellowship (remember, relationship means a personal investment of time).

When you hear the word *relationship*, what comes to mind? We all probably have a similar idea about what a relationship should be like. At one time in each of our lives, we have wanted to be in strong relationship with someone. We dream of the time when we'll find that special someone, that soul mate, and then when we find it (if we do), we go all out. We do anything to make the other person happy, and hope for the same in return. That is what makes a relationship work: give and take, trust, and the communication of ideas, values, and dreams. A relationship like this with a human soul mate happens only once in a lifetime, if we are lucky, and even then may not last forever. But with Christ, you can expect this kind of relationship to last until you meet him face to face.

For this reason, it is so very important to trust in God and keep up a relationship with him, because Jesus states that he will never leave or forsake you. He says that he will be your friend in times of need, as well as in times of plenty. Through thick and thin, no matter what, he is there for you. He can identify with whatever you are going through because he was actually here on earth, living the human experience. He has personal experience with life on life's terms. God allowed this to happen to him so that he would know what it was like to have to battle life and would be able to empathize with us, and have a real relationship with us.

So, if we are to have a one-on-one relationship with Jesus Christ, rather than a reliance on religion, is attending a church even necessary? Yes. But we must keep the role of Christ and the role of the church separate in our minds. We must realize what Jesus stated very clearly: that he alone is the door to eternal and abundant life; he should be our primary guide through life; and, when all is said and done, he alone is what truly matters in life. In essence, Jesus is the key to life. And through the Holy Spirit, he will be our ultimate inner guide, allowing us to be sensitive to the teachings of Jesus, spreading abroad the love of God in our hearts, and allowing us to know the wisdom of the ages.

On the other hand, church is where we go to fellowship with others of like mind, (i.e., the mind of Christ). Church is where we are to go to find relief from the world, gain sanctuary, and find peace of mind. Unfortunately, due to the legalism of religion, that perception of the church has been tarnished.

Church is just a building; it is only as good as its members. Members must be involved and spiritually healthy. (Spiritual health is imparted by the Holy Spirit through a relationship in which you gain knowledge of the Word by studying it.) The health of a church can be measured by its ability to welcome strangers and change the surrounding community, and by the power of the Holy Spirit that surrounds its individual members out in the world.

When you walk into a church, you should feel the Holy Spirit's presence. Peacefulness will surround the place, and after the sermon, you should come away having been taught or convicted of something. Why? Because the power of a church, as a whole, is directly related to the power of the Holy Spirit that is allowed by its member to flourish unhampered. The Holy Spirit is what guides the church in the direction it should be going. And if a church is not following that direction, or is just not in tune with the Holy Spirit, then it will die.

To change the image of church, we need to change the image of Christians. How Christians act and what they say within society—outside the church—is what the church is judged by. If they can pass those tests, then others might start being interested in going to church. It is their job to draw others into the church by example, going and reaching out to those whom religion will not.

I expect that if Jesus were on earth now, he would have almost the exact same experience with the church and with society. He would get the same reactions as he got then. The ruling Christian sect would act the same, having the same multimillion-dollar buildings, the same sense of piousness, the same sacrilegious views that were present two thousand years ago.

The same people in society would be ignored, too: the tax collectors, prostitutes, bikers, drug addicts, and low-income folks; the uneducated, the poor, and the homeless. Yet those folks have always been the true backbone of the people God calls. Why? These are the folks Jesus can work with because their pride isn't in the way. They know he can make their lives better and that they can have all things through Christ.

The church needs to be more like Christ. He is the way, the truth, and the light, and the members of the church are his disciples. They are the ones people watch. Their attitudes, issues, behaviors, and states of mind are the examples of Christ that people see. How they socialize and present themselves to others really matters. This is how the church is judged—by its members out in the community.

If you profess to be a Christian and are part of a church, remember that the Word says we will be known by our love. That means people should be able to tell we represent Christ just by how we treat others and by how much we care for those who are not in the church. Is our love visible? Do we walk what we preach? Do we stop and give others our time, regardless of whether they are involved with the church?

Jesus hung out in the slums and with those whom everyone knew were sinners. He tried to save the lost because he loved them and because he loved his father in Heaven. I believe this is also our mission. And to fulfill it, we need to be more into the Word—reading and studying it, and listening to others teach about it. This is what will allow us to be Jesus to others.

Nine: Compromise

Compromise is the number one offender in our lives. In fact, in the very meaning of the word *compromise* is the idea of settling for something that is less than. How many times do we justify doing something we know we shouldn't, saying to ourselves, "No one will find out," or, "It isn't that big of a deal." And then after we do it, we say, "If only I had not allowed myself to go there. I knew better!"

That's because compromise happens slowly, in little bits and pieces. It never happens in one big chunk, so large that you take notice. So compromise is more apt to happen with small issues that, at the time, seem insignificant, but in the end add up to catastrophe.

The good news is there is nothing new under the sun when it comes to the enemy's arsenal. All of the old weapons work well enough. Among these is what I call The Big Three. These are three major areas of our lives that, if we don't surrender them to God as we mature in him, are doomed to get us into trouble later on. The Big Three are:

1. The pride of life;
2. The lust of the flesh; and
3. The lust of the eye.

These are the biggest offenses of the Christian community, having taken down all of the major preachers that used to be on television. And they are the three areas that will get you and me, if we do not allow Jesus to work in us to remove them. That is why it is so important become ourselves spiritually fit, so we cannot be fooled into compromise.

We have to remember that no matter what, we are responsible for our actions, and no one else. We are the ones who decide what to do. We might have to decide between two very bad choices, but decide we must. Even choosing not to decide is a decision. Any time a decision must be made, we have a choice to do what we know is right, as hard as that may be, or to allow compromise to slip in and do what we know is not up to our, or God's, standards.

Even in matters with nothing on the line, we have to ask ourselves whether we are living to God's standards or choosing to set different ones. In fact, I find that the most inane situations are the easiest in which to allow compromise. In one such instance, the situation meant nothing, and there was no heavy consequence on the line, but I found myself lying. Later, I had to ask myself, "Why did I do that?"

The truth is, compromise happens in all our lives at one time or another. We just have to be ready to catch it when it does happen, admit it, ask forgiveness, and make a better choice the next time around. Although the thing about compromise is that it never happens the same way twice, so as we are ready for it to attack us from one direction, we don't see it coming at us from another. And, of course, it doesn't help matters that with the temptation to compromise comes the urge to rationalize and make excuses.

We always have a reason, don't we? We are always ready with an explanation about why we could not do the right thing. If we spent half the time being honest with ourselves as we did coming up with justification, we would save ourselves a lot of time and energy. You see, the decision to compromise usually happens in a split second, and then we spend the rest of our time second guessing ourselves, which is a form of torment designed by the enemy to enslave us farther. First, he tempts us, and then we feel condemnation for giving in. So we lose twice, just to do something we should not have been doing in the first place. It is like a dog chasing its tail: loads of energy expended for a whole lot of nothing (except for, of course, the amusement of those watching).

At the root of many compromise situations are taking shortcuts and being somewhere we are not supposed to be, or doing something we are not supposed to do. If you recall a time when you compromise, I'll bet you were somewhere you should not have been, doing or saying something you should not have been, or just trying to get out of something.

So, we can avoid compromising situations or at least make them easier to deal with by being sure of what we believe and knowing our motive for doing things. We need to be ever vigilant of our motive—the reasons we are doing something—and then ensure we are doing it for the right reason.

And if we are doing it for the wrong reason, then we need to be honest and allow ourselves to be wrong.

Some questions you might ask yourself in order to determine your motive are, "What is behind me acting this way or saying these things?" and, "Do I have the best interest of someone else in mind, or am I trying to make myself look better?"

Motives are the underlying issue in everything we do. Said another way, we do nothing without motive. Let me give you an example. In the beginning of my walk with God, it took me awhile to get out of the mindset that I had been conditioned to have on the streets, in which you did nothing for anyone else without expecting something in return. Sure, I would do for you, but then you went on the secret list of owing me. And, I never forgot. If you did not pay up, there was an issue with us, and I would get resentful and bent out of shape, to the point that I was fuming inside. (This, too, is a ploy of the enemy—getting us first to feel resentment, and then to justify it, evoking the sympathy of anyone who will listen to us rant about how wronged and cheated we are, and how horrible the other person is).

The worst instances of this were when I ranted about fellow Christians—those who were my very brothers and sisters in Christ—saying how un-Christian they were to have acted such a way. So, while I was gossiping, backbiting, and causing dissention just to get even, I was doing the same thing that I was accusing them of doing in the first place: being un-Christian.

To this day, there are times when I find myself doing things and expecting something in return. But the more I read, study, and meditate on the Word of God, the more I am convicted of and work on my wrong motives.

It's from personal experiences like these that I know how very important it is to be watchful for compromise. But compromise does not just affect us; it can affect others as well. As I mentioned earlier, the world will watch those of us who profess to be Christ like to see how we really act—not in church, but in real life. If they see you getting hostile and out of control, swearing, fighting, and being under the influence, they wonder what the point is. Why profess to be a Christian when you act just like everybody else? They then assume all Christians are all alike, and instead of getting converts to the faith, we turn people off. This is where the saying "I'd rather see a sermon than hear one any day" comes into play.

Is it fair that Christians are judged this way? No, of course not, but it happens everywhere you go; which is why it is so important to be able to live under the blood of Christ. Of ourselves, we can do nothing, but through him, all things are possible. And because of him, we are able to rise above the norm and get to the point where we are living like Christ because we want to, not because we have to.

This point where we go from being obligated to wanting to, the place where we serve Christ because of what he did for us and not because of our fear of going to hell, is the place where true love forms in our relationship with Jesus. This is where change happens. This is where the life we lead becomes more pleasurable, because we realize that it is the gift of ourselves that we are able to give him—our life, lived to him—in place of death. We find ourselves looking to Jesus for direction on purpose. We find that what God states in his word does happen, and so we begin to rely on it.

This love approaches slowly. At first, you may not be able to grasp it. You may wonder, "Why does God love me? Why does God care what happens to me? What business is it of his, anyway—that is, if there even is a God?" Then in one special moment, it arrives, and everything changes. You get a glimpse of what can be. You start to feel, maybe for the first time, that there is hope, that there is a future for you, and that it might not be as bleak as it appeared at first.

Then you find freedom. You see that the things Christ tells you to do and not do in his word are for your own safety, and that its lessons are there to help guide you along the path of salvation. Thus, you start to see the Bible as a love letter, all while being an instruction manual to you personally, that provides guidance, fellowship, and a blueprint for life.

The reason I am talking about this is because when love is left out of the equation, you know that compromise is about to take root. In fact, this is the very reason why we have religion in the churches, places that Christ originally formed out of love. Churches lost love and allowed compromise, and look what that has gotten us today: chaos and confusion, Christians killing each other, stating that one denomination is better than another.

In 1st Corinthians 13, it talks about what love looks like, and in love, there can be no compromise. Love is just what it is—nothing more, nothing less. Love is what prompted God to allow Jesus to come to earth as a sacrifice. Jesus is love personified. And as he walked this world, he preached love.

Compromise can't live with love because while love is perfect, compromise is defective. So you have to let go of what is pure and right to allow compromise to enter. And once compromise is left to grow, death is its only conclusion. Love demands that we look to another and ask, "What can I do for you"? And there is no compromise in that.

Ten: **Change**

It has been said that the definition of insanity is doing the same thing over and over again, but expecting different results. If you never do anything different in your life, then nothing different will ever happen to you. If you want change, you have to act differently. Otherwise, you will always get as you have always gotten; and, as you have likely figured out by now (or you wouldn't be reading this book), what you have always gotten is no longer acceptable to you.

You have to work at change, and it is uncomfortable, hard, humbling, and often painful, but then nothing worth getting is ever easily gotten. Change is especially difficult when we get older, because we become set in our ways, even if those ways are no longer working.

To start the change process, you must look at what has stopped working in your life and figure out what to do to get up off the ground, back in the driver's seat, and in full charge of your life—your attitude, your power, and your emotions. You will want to do this keeping in mind that your life should be built on a basis of love and the seven foundation principles: honor, dignity, respect, integrity, mercy, grace, and unmerited favor. Without these principles operating in your life, you are doomed from the beginning.

There are times in each of our lives when we just require more. We may not even know what we require more of, but we know that our lives are no longer working because of it. When we get to that point, where we can no longer ignore the trouble in our lives, we need to cry out to God to help us. And, because he is God, he will send help. Sometimes it is in the form of angelic intervention, or just a small feeling in your heart. Sometimes it comes in a dream. Sometimes a word from God comes from an outside source, such as a counselor, friend, family member, even a stranger. But no matter how help is delivered, rest assured God will provide it. That is his promise to us.

God promised that, as children of God, we have the ability to enter into his throne room, walk right up to the throne, and sit on the father's lap, to talk to him or just to be. Being adopted into the family of God gives us certain rights and privileges, as we become sons and daughters of the Most High. And the only thing he requires from us is a willingness to believe that all of this is possible. Remember, the only thing God cannot get from us is our free will. Free will is a precious gift from God, given so that we would heed his call and turn our will and life over to his care at the perfect time—when we understood him. God cannot force us to give him our lives as living sacrifices. He cannot even demand it. It has to be a free gift from us to him.

Then and only then can we come to him without spot or blemish, because he will have washed all our sins away. And it's all due to the bloodshed on the cross at Calvary. That one final act of total selflessness, giving his life, allows us to give our lives back to him. All we have to do is believe it is possible. As long as we believe that he can deliver us, that He can work in our lives, and that he cares about what happens to us, we are in a position to carry out his will. He can work in us, through us, and for us. He has given us all we need to follow him, all that we need to succeed in life, and all that we need to overcome the evil one; we just need to believe.

God can work in our life because he knows us, and he knows where we are in our walk with him. He knows how much we have suffered, and how much we fall short. He knew what he was getting when he called us. He did not turn to an angel and say, "Boy, I didn't see that one coming." It says in his word that he knew us in the womb, and that we were predestined to come to him. He also stated in John that he wished for all to come to him, know the glory of God, and be able to go to heaven. He did not wish for anyone to be left behind.

But we know that some refuse to believe that he is who he says he is, and thus choose not to accept him into their hearts. Unfortunately, they pay the ultimate price: eternity without hope, without light, and without the possibility of redemption and inclusion into the Kingdom of God.

After believing that God can save us and work in our life, the next step is to take action. This is why many say that, to Jesus, the word *faith* is a verb. It states in Ephians that "faith without works is dead." (Ephians

2:9)If you look at any miracle preformed in the word of God, you will find that action accompanied it. In both the old and new testaments, when a person wanted a miracle, he, or someone in his family, went to go get it. Likewise, if we want a miracle, we have to go get it. In other words, we need to actively seek whatever it is—whatever change—we need from God.

Your action of faith, your action toward change, might be buying this book, reading it, accepting Christ into your life, and going to your local full- gospel church and getting involved. If you have not accepted Christ into your life, and you wish to do so, just say this prayer and mean it with all your heart:

> *Jesus, I know that I am a sinner. I know that by myself, I am not able to make a single thing happen. I know that I have done things, said things, and behaved in ways that were not positive. I have done things that I am not proud of, and I am in a place where I can't seem to get a grip on my life. I am asking you, Jesus, to come into my life, to forgive me for my sins, and to help me understand what I am doing, where I am going, and how you want me to proceed. I can no longer do this by myself. I need your help to go on. I am asking you to take away my sins and to be the lord and master of my life. I want to do things your way from now on. I believe that your blood was shed at the cross for my sins, that you rose again on the third day, and that you went into hell, beat the devil, and got the keys to death. I believe that you are looking out for me, and that you know me, love me, and want me. I believe that from this day on, I am a new creature in Christ, that my old self has passed away, and that my name is now written in the Lamb's Book of Life. Thank you, Jesus, for hearing me.*

And that is all there is to it. You are now a born-again Christian. That means that instead of religion, you now have a personal relationship with Christ. It means that all of the old things in your life are gone, and everything is new. There is an actual celebration going on in heaven right now, just because of you. The Bible states that when one who is lost becomes found, heaven rejoices.

But now it is up to you to go and find guidance. There will be some full-gospel churches in your area. Look in the phone book, ask around, or drive around, and find one that you can be comfortable with and that preaches the true word of God. You can also go to my church's Web site to receive a newsletter and more information about what it means to be a new creature in Christ. www.1livinghope.com

Now that is the biggest change that you can make: going from death to life. And as we proceed, we will see that change need not be a monster; it need not be this horrible thing from which we want to run. Change is good. It allows us to get from Point A to Point B. It is the catalyst from which all greatness is born. Yes, change is uncomfortable, and yes, it is sometimes scary, but if done with the guidance of Jesus, and without reservation, it is always rewarding. Christ will never take us where we can't go. He will never lead where we can't follow. There may be times when we think we can't do something, but that is just a lie to keep us where we are.

Eleven: **The Compost Heap**

What is a compost heap? In short, it is a pile of rotting, stinking refuse that, eventually, can be used for good. You create a compost heap by throwing natural, biodegradable garbage (e.g., bad or half-eaten fruit, or landscaping materials such as wood chips) into a pile.

Garbage is arranged in layers by type, and over time, as more and more layers accumulate, the things on the bottom start to decompose—in other words, rot—and turn into fertilizer, which you can then use in your yard or garden. You usually find compost heaps in the backyard, hidden in a corner away from everything, because of the stench they eventually produce.

Essentially, the compost heap "cooks" from the inside out; as the materials age, they rot and melt together, cooking from the bottom layer up until it becomes something else entirely different than what it was when it began.

A compost heap is much like our life when we allow ourselves to bury our problems—our garbage—instead of dealing with them. Unfortunately, when we try to push our issues out of our minds, they do not go away; instead, they just become buried in our psyche. Oh, that pile of garbage may be hidden from our view for a while, just like that compost heap in the corner of the backyard, and of course, out of sight, out of mind. But soon it starts to rot and produces a stench that is unignorable.

Finally, it starts to turn into something entirely different. The things buried at the very bottom start to cook, and if we do not ask God to help us remove it and use it for good, it comes out sideways, affecting our behaviors and attitudes for the worse. Things buried alive never die.

In the Word of God it clearly states that, as new creatures in Christ, old things will pass away. Therefore, we must get to a place in our lives where we are willing to ask Christ to remove these buried things. And as most garbage has usually been buried for quite some time, it often takes help from an outside source to start to uncover it. Once we do, however, God can help us remove it and, if we let him, will use it to grow new life elsewhere. And it is at this point, as it states in Ephesians, that we are transformed by the renewing of our minds—or, said another way, by our new attitudes.

Most of us have probably gone through life attempting to keep up with the Joneses. And just keeping up is usually not enough for Type A personalities, who like to be first in everything, no matter what it takes. But this kind of attitude is what often causes us to make excuses for our behaviors, to justify our actions, to live a lie by pretending that everything is okay even when it is not. We rationalize to make our conscience go away, and then bury the residual guilt. Sometimes we even bury the memory of what we have done, trying to trick our minds into believing it never happened. And so over time, out of pride and self-defense, we become very efficient compost heap builders. And the more we bury, the more we push down the layers underneath, until something's got to give.

Often it happens unexpectedly. One day, you will be going along just fine, and then for no apparent reason, you blow up at someone or get into a bad mood. You're puzzled, because there appears to be nothing wrong on the surface. But underneath, all hell is breaking loose. The garbage of your life that you have buried is starting to come out sideways.

So, can you understand why the way we view things now is directly related to our past? What we buried then affects how we see things now. How we approach a situation today depends on what we went through in our many yesterdays. The way in which a person without hidden issues approaches an incident will be drastically different than that of someone else, who has been through the ringer and become hardened by life. The person who has a clean slate inside will tend to view situations with gentleness, calmness, and a softness of spirit, whereas someone with a jaded spirit will see them totally differently. This is how we can get ten different recollections from ten different people viewing the same event.

No matter what we have been through, though, we can let go of our past, releasing all of the guilt, pride, hostility, and resentment that goes along with it, and allow healing—but only as much as we let God in. During what can be the long process of uncovering buried garbage and transforming it into something good, it's not unusually for skepticism to set in. We may begin to question how much Jesus can actually do for us, especially if we see God working in others' lives, while ours still feels stagnant. To combat such doubt, remember that God can only work as much as we let him. Also keep in mind that God may well be working in us, but because we often cannot see ourselves objectively enough to notice subtle changes, we feel there is none.

Remember that the Holy Spirit, Jesus, and God are all gentlemen. They will never force themselves into a life to which they were not invited. So, it becomes totally up to us how much work Jesus can do in us, and how much healing will occur. It is up to us to comply with Jesus and the work he is trying to do, even though we may at first feel very resistant to it—because, however sick this sounds, there are times in everyone's lives when the insanity we have become used to seems more comfortable than the uncertainty of a new and improved life.

You see, we can grow so familiar with something over time, even the stench of a compost heap, that we actually become afraid to get rid of it. Depending on how long something has been buried, or the impact of the buried event on us (e.g., how traumatic it was, or the emotional toll it took on us), we may find ourselves struggling to hang on to the pain or anger or guilt. We may even use the traumatic events as excuses to condone our current, albeit unattractive, behavior. But when the student is ready, the teacher will appear.

When we are ready to let go, the Holy Spirit will place someone in our life who has a similar past and can help us wade through the scary, unknown waters toward healing. These people can help guide us in the right direction—*through* the issue, rather than under, over, or around it, as we'll be inclined to do to avoid the pain. After all, avoidance is how things became buried in the first place. Going through the issue, facing it head on, involves dealing with all of the emotions, stress, and negative thoughts that have built up over time, but it will get us to a point where we can leave it all behind once and for all. And that brings us to the next chapter, which just happens to be about forgiveness.

Twelve: **Forgiveness**

We all resent something or another in our past, and we may just not be ready or not know how to let go. But Jesus is able and willing to forgive us of any sin we have committed, no matter how horrible we feel it is. On that same token, Jesus told us that we can let go of anything, because he took all of the punishment for our sins on the cross. He did that so that we could forge forward and complete the race he has set before us, following the calling he has put on our lives.

In fact, as soon as we come to Christ, the past is forgiven, and we can be 100 percent sure that a new life awaits us. Who we were and what we have done no longer counts against us, as Jesus has removed our sin from us as far as "the East is from the West," (Ps.103:12)and thrown it into the sea of forgetfulness. We are new creatures in Christ, no longer bound by the law of sin and death, but under the law of the spirit of life (Romans 6–8). If you're interested in knowing more on this topic, know that Paul spends a lot of time in the book of Romans detailing how to be delivered; stay delivered, and walk in forgiveness. Suffice it to say here, if we can learn to do all that, we have the key to life.

There is only one requirement for receiving forgiveness from Christ: we must forgive ourselves and others. The word states that if we are not able to forgive others, Christ will not forgive us. And to be able to forgive others, we must have love. First Corinthians 13 is the Bible's blueprint for what love should look like, and it says that love never holds grudges or remembers wrongs done to it. But we humans like to hold onto grudges, as it gives us an excuse to get back at others who have hurt us. It gives us license to do unto others before they do unto us, and to even the score, thus effectively cutting out God.

But the word says only Jesus has the authority to right wrongs, to meet out justice, and to get retribution on others, so we should be leaving it all to him. This is a hard thing to do, especially when we are used to handling things ourselves. But once we are saved, Christ becomes the center of our lives and promises to defend and protect us, so we must hand over every part of our lives to him. As we mature in him, this process becomes easier, as we learn from experience that he always does a much better job with these things than we could ever do.

Another thing to keep in mind is that forgiving isn't a feeling; it's a choice. It seems to me that we always want to *feel* like forgiving someone before we actually take that step. We think, "When I feel like I can forgive them, I will," or, "I just can't get what they did out of my head; I don't think I'll ever be able to forgive them." What we're forgetting is that we need to choose to forgive, regardless of how we feel. We can make that choice by softening our hearts to realize that given everything for which God has forgiven us, who do we think we are that we should not forgive another?

How do we then become willing to make the choice to forgive? This is the crucial step. Willingness has to start with a "heart condition." A heart condition is a realization that our way isn't working, that we are just getting more miserable with time, and that our life just isn't running as it should. You've most likely heard this heart condition called *conviction*. Through conviction, we soften to the Word of God. It's almost like tenderizing meat: if you beat it enough, the meat's toughness goes by the wayside, but then it becomes melt-in-your-mouth delicious. If we have given our lives over to him completely, then we will receive conviction through the Holy Spirit.

That's because God truly sees us and knows us. This is one reason that we can't just play church. We can't just do our own thing Monday through Saturday, and then act all pious on Sunday, and if we are feeling truly magnanimous, even on Wednesday night. God sees our heart and our motives even better than we do. So when we get to that point where we feel things are just not quite right, or when we feel that uneasiness that comes through the still, small voice of conviction, we can know that it is God speaking to us, leading us from where we've strayed back to the straight and narrow path. But I believe that conviction and forgiveness go hand in hand, so where there is conviction, know that forgiveness is not far behind.

Conviction and forgiveness are not normal animal responses. In the animal world, there is no forgiveness; there are just consequences that occur with instinct and survival. Only with Christ are our normal animal instincts quelled. The word states that God has directed our life since the creation of time that a plan was in place before we were even born. So we must listen for him, and allow him to take our lives and mold them according to his will.

So the bottom line of forgiveness is first willingness and then choice. Are we willing to allow Christ to work in our lives more than we are willing to hang onto our past? We often make the mistake of believing that we are the ones at the helm of the ship of life, but in order to be forgiven by him, we must be willing to get right with God, since he is the one who endows us with the willingness in the first place.

Thirteen: **Choice**

Choice is a big deal. It is the only gift you're given for a lifetime. When a choice is in front of you, whether you make a decision or not, you are choosing, since even *not* choosing is a choice. Regardless of whether we choose, we must live with the consequences, and that is the part that gets us most, isn't it? Having to live with the choices we have made?

When I started using I was eleven or twelve years old. Everyone I knew at that time was already using, too, but then those were the people I chose to hang out with. I chose my friends and I chose to obey or disobey. Even at that young age, I had some idea of what was going on around me. Enough of an idea that it would not be fair to say I was forced; I followed the crowd. There others I knew who chose not to follow the crowd, regardless of how hard it must have been for them.

As I got older and my lifestyle changed, I found myself, like everyone else at this age, facing choices every day. It is around this age when we have a choice to follow directions or go our own way. A choice to follow the crowd or stand on our own; a choice to have sex or remain a virgin and a choice to do drugs or not. In any given situation, we have a choice. We may have really bad options to choose from, but we still have a choice.

We also all reach a certain point in our life when we sense God calling us, and again we have a choice to listen or not. We have a choice to enter into God's family and become involved in a local church. Then, later, a choice to join a prayer group, Bible study, or home support-group. And what will our choice be? Will we choose to listen to that small, still voice that we call God or our conscious, or will we ignore it and accept the consequences that ensue?

The funny thing about choices is that you have to figure out what your choices are before you can make a decision. In Today's world, most of us can name someone who is addicted to something, whether it be shopping, alcohol, drugs, gambling, sex, video games, the Internet—you name it, and there is a support group for it someplace. Most addicts refuse to look too long and hard at choices, however, because it confuses them. If they look at alternatives too hard, they actually might not go out and relapse again, they might stand and change. Most addicts have their minds set before getting involved with their respective addictions, so they plan to relapse, they know what they are going to do before they do it, it's just those surrounding the addict that hold out hope time after time..

Any addict knows that he is going to relapse before he actually does it. You can talk until you're blue in the face, but he will not look at any other choice once his mind is made up. That is called habit. Before an addict goes on a run is the point in the process when it is generally the hardest to interject other options, but it is also the point when offering those ideas will do the most good. In fact, this is one of the principles that twelve-step programs are based on—replacing old ideas with new ones, in essence, replacing the old habit with the new "habit" of thinking positively. I think of it like a mental CD player. As soon as the old CD starts playing in the addict's head, telling her that she won't make it without a fix, is the very time when a new CD—one stating that she is better than her addition, that she does not need a fix but can allow God to get her through instead—needs to be handed to her. But she must choose to play it.

The decision I make every morning is to follow Christ, because I know what my life was like without him. If figure that from that point on, I can follow Jesus, or go the way of the world; everything else in life stems from those two choices. Like Paul states in the Bible, life is like running a race, so why run if not to win?

In turn, the goals I choose to go after for the day are determined by the choices I make in the morning. So if I choose to walk with Christ, I will set goals such as I want to learn as much as I can, I want to talk to someone new, I want to follow directions, I want to go to a meeting, I want to talk to someone in my support group. I want to do those things. Those are my goals if I choose Christ.

One of the most important goals, I think, for anyone who chooses to follow Christ every morning is to be open to reaching out to others. When I go to a meeting, for example, I want to look for someone new, especially someone who may appear uncomfortable or insecure or scared, and stick my hand out in welcome. As a born-again, Spirit-filled Christian, I feel that is my job. I am not talking about being a counselor; I am just talking about being a family member of the Christ family.

As I see it, it is the job of every Christian to make the newcomer feel welcome, because if we don't, a newcomer is libel to just turn and walk out the door. I know this because someone did it for me, and it worked wonders. These days, we've all had enough of phony Christians—those who put on an act in the beginning, but when you get to know them, they are no better than the people they're professing to try to save. So when you have the opportunity to meet and help people genuinely, you must take it. You give the newcomer a *choice* by putting your hand out and saying, "I'm Steve Shafer. I'm glad you are here." You give him the chance, and the choice, to say, "I'm Joe Blo. I'm glad I am here, too."

In the long run, you may have given the newcomer the choice to live or to die, which is talked about in Deuteronomy 29–31, followed by the instruction to "choose life." As a Christian, you have the opportunity to pass such a choice off to them, and that is deep; think about that for a minute. Giving life away is the way it is supposed to be. That is how Christ and the disciples did it.

There is something that happens to you when you give your life over to Christ. And people become attracted to that something, because it changes everything in you and shines in your life. And because it was your choice, it gives you self-esteem. You feel good about the choice you made, which, in turn, makes you feel good about yourself. And when you feel good about yourself, you will make better choices for the rest of your life.

Do you see how the choice to allow Jesus into your life gains momentum and snowballs into other good life choices? Someone had the decency to give you the choice of life or death in the beginning—the choice to accept Christ or not.

On this same token, there are ways to give away your choice. When you turn your back on God, or when you say there is no hope or no faith; when you give your inner self over to depression, anger, denial, or hate. These are all ways to relinquish choice. You can also turn over your choice to your bartender, your dealer, or your bookie, or to shopping, eating, impure sex, or gambling. And how, by doing this, do you feel relieved? How does harming yourself make things better? It doesn't, of course. It makes things worse. But then that is the plan of the enemy—to get you to a point where you become totally ineffective. Then the enemy does not have to worry about what damage you can do.

The minute you give away your choice, you are no longer a human being. You are an animal. Such a mindless existence might work for a while, but in the end, no matter who you are, what you have, or where you go in life, there is a four o'clock in the morning, and that is when the truth comes out. In that moment; when no one but you and God are there to witness your demise

It is in this moment, when you choose to get help, that the enemy is defeated.

Then, hopefully, you make the choice to pull out and walk with Christ. Luckily, the word of God is what gives you that choice. The word of God is the foundation on which you can change your life. That's because for every problem you might encounter, there is an answer in the Word of God.

Once you've decided to change, the next choice to make is in regard to what area of life to concentrate on first. To make that choice, you must ask yourself, "Where do I feel most out of whack?" And, as you pray, Jesus will point out those areas he feels need work, usually by allowing something to happen to you that you cannot ignore.

Once you have decided which area in your life to focus on, the next choice to make is to do the work necessary to change. A lot of times we want to make changes only if it does not hurt too bad or become too uncomfortable, so we must make the choice to change wholeheartedly, no matter the effort involved. But there is a catch. To really make life-giving changes to ourselves is a decision that can only be done with the help of Jesus. We have already seen that we alone cannot get it right. But coupled with Christ, we will choose to win every time.

Yes, there will be hard times. Yes, you will get stripped of everything you hold dear, including attitudes, thoughts, perspectives, and behaviors that do not line up with the Word of God. But just remember that to break a habit is a choice. Each and every day, it's your choice to follow the right path or not.

An important thing to mention is that you cannot just stop the behavior itself. You must change what is at the root of the behavior, uproot it, and replace it with Christ. Otherwise, the addiction will just pop out somewhere else. You may not do drugs anymore, but you have sex 24-7. You may not drink anymore, but you gamble or work eighty-five hours a week because you did not address the real problem. But if you just switch addictions, you are still an addict.

Christ like living is a decision of serenity. But if you're like I was, you do not know what peace is. You have been in turmoil so long that if there is not a crisis going on, you think the world is coming to an end. If there is not a major issue to be fixed or a major incident that throws everything into chaos, then you think something must be wrong.

I will never forget the first time I had a normal day. I had no highs and no lows. I had no big decisions to make and no chaos, and I had not made anyone angry. I called up some people from my support group and said, "I am losing it! And I am depressed—nothing is happening." To my surprise, I received assurance that this is what normal was all about—to have no life-threatening issues ready to collapse my life—and that this is what we were working toward as our life goal. Serenity and calmness was normal and the way it was supposed to be. The word states that we are to be calm, pleasant-minded, and in control at all times. But at the time, that was a foreign idea to me.

One guy I called even told me, "If you want excitement, parachute out of an airplane or bungee off a bridge. Just something to give you that rush, if that's what you need. Just don't go back to that life you lived before, getting all caught up in perfection. Only one person was perfect, and they hung him on a cross, so I think I'll stay away from that."

I had to argue with myself for about the first three or four months after I gave my life back to Christ, because I truly thought that my life was over. I thought all Christians were dull and boring. And I thought all Christians were hypocrites. Unfortunately for me, the enemy would put people into my life that affirmed this concept—Christians who were double-minded, unsure of themselves, and weak. I wanted to be self-assured, self-aware, strong, unwavering when in trouble, and able to handle myself in times of need. And I had never met a Christian like that.

It took ten years of being in the Alcoholic Anonymous and Narcotic Anonymous programs to get to the point where I would give Christ a real try and that was only because my life was falling apart. My marriage was in the toilet, my kids were on drugs, and I had been declared disabled after being hit by a drunk driver. There was a lot going on in my life and I knew something had to change. I had had a relationship with Christ throughout my life, but had never stuck with it.

Until that point, I never fully appreciated the serenity and joy that came with a life dedicated to Christ. I have been walking with Christ for six and a half years now, and he has asked me to go places I never dreamed, and asked me to give up things that I said I never would. There is still a battle going on, but I know that without Christ, my life is nothing. Without Christ, I don't even have the choice to move forward, to reach my goals, and to have peace. I need Christ in my life to show me the way to go to fulfill my destiny in him.

Still, effort is required to maintain a Godly life. As mentioned before, a good way to do this is to get involved in a church, a Bible study, and some form of prayer group. But I also suggest that, as soon as you pick a church, going twenty minutes early and staying twenty minutes late. When you show up early, you will be able to meet the people who are most involved. They'll be the ones setting up and ushering. The worship team and the pastors will probably also be there. Out of, say, a hundred people who attend the service, this handful of people are often the most dedicated. Thus, they are people you want to stretch your hand out to, so that you, too, can learn to get involved. Because when you are involved, you have more of a stake, and you are more likely to go.

You will also be more likely to go because getting involved in this way will prevent you from using one of the age-old excuses for not sticking with church: "I do not know anyone." If you want any degree of success in your walk with God, you cannot come in late, sit in the back, and shoot out before the service is over so that you won't have to meet anyone. If you do not let anyone in church get to know you because you don't want to be held accountable by anyone else, God already knows that—so be honest with yourself and reach out to him for help.

Besides, if you go late and leave early just to avoid getting close to people, you will likely not enjoy the service or meeting as much, or get the full benefit of the message or teaching being delivered—and that, too, can become an excuse to stop going: "These meetings stink. I am not getting anything meaningful out of them when I go." Of course you won't get anything out of them, because you are not present and available for things to happen.

By going early and leaving late, you will also put yourself in a position where you are instantly associating and making friends with people who tend to be steadier in their walks with God, and who make the right choices in their lives. In other words, you will become a part of the right "click." Yes, there are clicks in church, and do not let anyone tell you there aren't. Also, don't think that everyone in the same church or even the same prayer group like one another all the time, and that you have to agree with every message or teaching. I have been to a lot of meetings that I did not like with people I did not like. And, believe you me, there are people in my church who do not like me. But, there are also bunches of people who do, and these are ones I seek out for friendships, because I have a choice today.

The word confirms this experience. It says that there will be times when I do not like everyone I meet, and when not everyone who meets me will like me. But it also says that I have to love everyone with the love that Jesus gives me. In fact, in the end, I will be judged by the amount of humility, love, and forgiveness I choose to give. (That fact used to frighten me, as I cut very little slack to others, although, to be fair, I cut myself even less. But, as mentioned earlier, this is among the many lessons in forgiveness that I am learning more and more about every day.)

Take a fearless moral inventory of yourself to know who you are. Watch your actions to make sure what you are saying and what you are doing match up, because you can bet others are. Likewise, and especially if you are young in your walk with Christ, take an inventory of others. See if they match their actions and words, and then use that information to decide whether they are people you would want to be involved your life. Remember, you have a choice.

Taking an inventory of someone else to be careful that you do not fall into a bad crowd is only prudent, sensible, and quite frankly justifiable, just so long as that is your motive. Because if you don't, you're at risk for falling into a crowd who will lead you back to sin, rather than you leading them to Christ—yes, these types of crowds exist even in the church. It is not okay, however, to assonate someone's character for the sake of warning people away from them—that is gossip, which Jesus states is in no way acceptable.

By getting involved with the right people, you learn that you do not have to carry around the garbage of your past all alone. That, too, is a choice. Because of my past, I thought I was so different from everyone else at my church, so bad, until I started talking to other people and found out they were as bad or worse. Then, I realized, "Hey, maybe I am not so bad after all." You cannot get such reassurance, though, until you get to know other people of like mind, all following Jesus.

You see, until we begin to reach out to others, all of us tend to think that we are the only ones with dirty little secrets, and therefore unworthy of being a part of God's family. But it is just this sense of shame that the enemy uses to get you to give up church and go back into sin. The reality is that none of us are as unique in our sin. If it has a name, then it has been done before—you are not the first. So you are always off the hook. It's the whole reason Christ forgives us the minute we ask him to, removing our sins from us as far away as the East is from the West.

One thing to remember as you become involved with others is that whenever you put yourself out there, you are opening yourself to both empathy and feedback. So when you trust someone enough to let them in on what is happening in your life, you need also to be responsible enough to listen to what comes back, even if it is not what you want to hear. If you have sought your friends wisely, then the feedback you get from them will likely be something you need to hear. Jesus speaks through people.

Likewise, if we hear something from God during our prayer time, we should choose to listen. Christ will never lead us the wrong way, and if you love yourself enough, then you'd better be ready to hear the truth. Feedback is part of love. So we should always choose to hear it and, at least, consider it.

We as Christians have to do this life thing together. Even the person with only one day as a born-again Christian has some insight into what God has provided her. We just all have to have enough self-respect and self-esteem to put ourselves out there, and make a change. You see, once our secrets are out, they no longer have power over us. A secret is a secret because of its power over us. So if I tell you something about me that I had been keeping secret, it cannot control me anymore. If it cannot control me anymore, it has no power over me. So in the end, it means nothing.

Of course, no discussion of choice is complete without talking about amends. Making amends does not mean telling everyone your life's story and saying you're sorry for the ten thousandth time. Sorry in itself doesn't mean a thing. But your lifestyle does. As such, making amends is about making a one-hundred-and-eighty-degree turnaround in behavior.

To make amends with yourself, you admit what you've done, forgive yourself, and ask for Jesus to change you. By doing this, you give yourself a choice. It is also wise to ask the others in your life for forgiveness after it becomes apparent that real change has occurred, this only is done through time.If you make an amends with yourself and begin to live life differently, you give yourself a choice. And by making the right choices, you give yourself confidence that you can do more, which helps you to continue on the path of positive change. Also, it is important to communicate the change in your life if necessary. We do not want people to think we are callous. One thing that occurs with Christ like behavior is a willingness to make amends both verbally and behaviorally.

Yes, it is easier to just sit somewhere on Sunday morning and listen to an inspirational message about how you can have anything you want in Christ. But there are conditions that apply for this truth to take effect, and unfortunately, not a lot of churches make that clear. There are too many Christians out there who become disappointed, because the wealth and prosperity they were "promised" did not come their way. Or, maybe they followed the guidelines once or twice and nothing changed, so they gave up, believing it was all a lie, and falling by the wayside.

But let me tell you, when it comes to being a Christian, success is not the default; it is gained through good choices and hard work. I know, because following Christ is the hardest thing I have ever done, bar none. But it is also the most rewarding.

Fourteen: **Motives**

Your motive is the reason you do something. It's what drives you to make the decisions you make, meet the people you meet, take the jobs you take, and raise your children the way you do. In general, motive is the reason we behave in certain ways. So motive can be either pure or impure.

Here's an example. I have offered to help you and would even like to be a close friend. Under normal circumstances, those behaviors would appear to be positive, but let's just say that you happen to be a millionaire. With this extra bit of information, the *reason* I want to help you comes into question. If my reason for helping and befriending you is only to get to a point where I'll be able to ask you for money and expensive things, and have you give them to me, my motives are impure. On the other hand, if I offer my help freely just because it is the right thing to do, and I never ask for or even expect anything in return, my motives are pure.

We need to keep our motives in check at all times because they have a direct correlation with our spirituality. Whenever we do something for the sole reason that we enjoy doing it, we have a pure motive; that is, we are doing it with a right spirit. If I sing, write, eat, or whatever, and the reason I am doing it is for the sheer joy of doing it, then I am lining up with the Word of God. The spirituality lies in being able to offer something to someone without expecting anything in return. The gift itself—of music, friendship, money, time, or togetherness—is just a byproduct. And if my motives are right as I give these gifts, as an extra bonus, I also feel better about myself.

On the other hand, what do I feel when I give with an impure motive? In other words, if I give only to expect something in return—but then you do not give me something in return? I feel a horrible, long-lasting resentment. Resentment is the byproduct of working from my ego, and if I am working from my ego, I cannot possibly be coming from a pure, spiritual place. Let's get real! If you are trying to con, manipulate, cheat, steal, lie, or in any other way play the game, the last thing on your mind is spiritually.

The reason for this is that you cannot have two opposing ideas in the same place. You cannot have love and hate in the same place, or goodness and corruption. So, if you are coming from a place of corruption or impurity, it is impossible for your motive to be pure.

Let me give you another example. A true musician writes his music because he enjoys writing music. He does not do it just to get a royalty, even though a royalty would be nice as an added bonus. Doing the thing for enjoyment is acting with a pure motive.

Now apply this idea to friendship. It is not what you can suck dry from your friends that is important. When someone needs your help, it is important that you help her just because you want her to get better. You want to see something positive happen in her life.

It is the same thing in your walk with Christ; if you are a "Christian" with an ulterior motive, you will fail; that is one reason so many Christians have a hard time sticking with it—because their motives are not pure. So ask yourself, why do you go to church or even profess to walk with Christ? Is it because your boss wants you to? Or are you here because your wife wants you here, or for your kids? Things at home are just getting too hot to handle, and you know this will shut them up for a while? Whatever the reason, if the core motive you are here is not because you want to change your life, then you will fail and fall back into sin. You will find an excuse—it is not hard! You wake up, just decide to no longer follow him, and out into the world you go. The problem with such a wavering attitude (e.g., following him one day but not the next), is that it makes you, according to the Word of God, "lukewarm." Christ states that if you are lukewarm, he will spew you from his mouth, and in my book, spewing is never a good thing.

One reason we need to keep our motives in check is because where we are coming from directly relates to where we are going. That is deep—you need to file that one away in mind! So, if I am coming from a place that is impure, then where I am going will also be impure. If I am starting from a place of deceit, anger, resentment, hatred, or denial, then how can that path possibly lead me to a place of spiritually, recovery, openness, and honesty? It cannot.

That is why we must ask ourselves, every day, where we are coming from. Are we coming from a place of love or from a place in the world? When I wake up in the morning, am I trying to get myself right spiritually, or am I trying to get over? The answers to those questions will dictate where I will go that day. It will dictate why I do things as well as how I do them.

Have you ever had one of those bad days? One of those days when people are just not doing what you expect them to, and the little things are aggravating you, shortening your tolerance and acceptance level by the minute? Sometimes there are uncontrollable circumstances that cause a bad day, but what about those days when there is no apparent reason for feeling bad? The next time you have one of those, look at where you started that day. Did you start from a place of impurity, a place that was not focused on Christ? If you did, then you got exactly what you set out for—misery.

Fortunately, you can start your day over anytime you want. You can stop your bad day, evaluate where you were coming from, and in your quiet place shoot up a prayer that helps you change course. You can start your day over as many times as you need until you get it right; that is the nature of walking with Christ. He gives us the grace, love, and forgiveness to change direction and keep going, and there is nothing we can do to earn it or be entitled to it. It is a free gift, available only through Jesus.

We, as Christians, must always be on alert for the thief that comes to "kill, steal, and destroy, for if you knew what time the thief was coming you would be able to prevent him from taking anything." Getting to a point where you regularly nip the enemy at the bud at the beginning of each day is a process.

I have learned that I have a couple of options to help me if I wake up in a really bad mood. Either I'll call someone—a five-minute chat with a brother in Christ before work can do wonders for my day—or I'll get on my knees and stay there until I feel I have a better attitude, or read the Bible. And what works each day will be different, because each morning you start anew. When you wake up, things that bothered you yesterday may not bother you today. But if you start with Christ, he will give you positive guidance no matter what the issue.

Ninety-five percent of the things that happen to us is perceived through our attitudes; only five percent is the actual occurrence. If someone says something negative to me, and my attitude stinks, then I will perceive the experience as negative and run with it. Likely, everything else that happens from there on out will appear negative. In that instance, I have chosen to get angry, upset, and frazzled because I haven't tried to change my perception, or do anything about it. I haven't called anyone, or done any reading or praying, and as such, I have stated to the spiritual world that I am willing to accept into my life anything it throws my way, no matter how negative.

But if, instead, I take a moment and turn my negative perception of that same bad event into something that I can experience in a positive light, the experience itself will then become positive. This is why it is so important to get into a positive frame of mind as quickly as possible after something negative happens. When you don't, the experience can color everything you perceive thereafter.

Each time I can view a negative event in a positive light, I gain confidence and security, both in myself and in Christ. I become more comfortable with me, as I know that I am trying to do the right thing for the right reason. And after a while, anything negative you may say to me won't matter. You can call me names, write grievances about me, gossip, and rally others against me, but I will let it go because I started from a place that has Christ as its center, not a place that the world dictates. And if I didn't start there, I can start there now.

This is a major area in the Christian lifestyle where the rubber meets the road. If I claim to be in a relationship with Jesus, then my life better show it right here, because it is not what we say, but what we do as Christians that count. Actions do speak louder than words. So I can say all this wonderful stuff about my relationship with Christ and then go back to my office and be a miserable man, not doing the work that I am supposed to be doing. Then, when people start to call, my attitude stinks, which affects everyone I speak to. All the people I have talked to are then bent out of shape, and pass that bad mood along to others. And all because I am not doing what I am supposed to do to achieve my personal best for my day's walk with God. Imagine how long this could continue, until someone spoke up and stated the obvious: get off the phone, get on your knees, and seek God.

But again, our words and actions cannot align until we work on the root problem: our motives and our resulting attitude. Sin is a disease of the attitude, and it's intelligent; it knows how to trip us and keep us focused on thoughts of ourselves and thoughts that are negative. That's why

Christianity is designed to deal with our attitudes and thinking, because these are at the core of our happiness and serenity. Yet Christianity takes time because it is a learned thing. Just as we learned to be really good sinners, we need to learn to be really good saints, and both lessons take time to set in.

You cannot be responsible for something you do not know. And once you do know that you have an option in how you act, you will usually act in the right manor, as very few people choose to be miserable.

Once you identify what your motives are, you need to determine what they should become, which may require whole new sets of questions, such as these:

- Do you want your family or significant other back? Do you want your house back? Or your money? Do you want your self-respect back?
- Do you want trust? Hope? Faith? Love?
- Do you really want to do the right thing? Do want to get better? Do you really want yourself back?

If you are truly tired of coming from a dead place, then you will do what you have to do to change with Jesus' help. If that means going to seven church meetings a week, then that's what you have to do. If it means leaving a job or an unhealthy relationship, or even changing your whole lifestyle or living environment, then you will just have to do it. If you truly want those things mentioned above, you will do whatever it takes to get them.

Then, once you've determined what you're shooting for, you figure out how to go about changing so that you can achieve these new motives. Nine times out of ten, the best first step is just to give up, give in, and surrender, realizing you are teachable. Because the moment you think you know it all, or the moment you have an answer for everything, is the moment you become defensive. And if you are planning a defense, you are already intent on sinning.

I've talked about this before, but it cannot be said enough that excuses are terrible. They try to make it alright for you to sin, and this applies not only to your external behavior but also to your internal attitudes and motives. You are not going to learn anything when you are too busy formulating an answer to a question that has not even been asked yet. Someone gets three or four words out of their mouth, and you are already forming a defense to explain why he is wrong and you are right. That is ego, which grows from pride.

I think this issue is particularly difficult for the America male population to address. We as a male society have been taught that emotion is a sign of weakness—unless that emotion is resentment, anger, or hatred. You see, those feelings are considered okay for a man to have. So it is okay to be angry but not to be afraid. And if you are afraid, you should turn that fear into anger.

Further, even when you are angry, it's not okay to say, "You know, I am angry," let alone, "I am confused, afraid, or upset, and I do not know what to do." Expressing feelings is unacceptable for a guy, and any guy who doesn't heed this unspoken rule is then labeled as a freak or a queer. If you are angry, it is only acceptable to lash out and to screw up.

Screwing up is okay for men to do too. It is okay to blunder into something and force your way through it. A real man would rather drive around for three hours in a neighborhood he does not know than to stop at a gas station and ask for directions. Even the media chooses to portray men in such an incompetent manner. Fictional men of TV are either too stupid, or too fat and lazy to get out of their own way, forcing wives to come to the rescue of these bumbling idiots.

This is what the generation of kids now is seeing; no wonder no one has respect for fatherhood anymore. This is a design by the enemy to discredit men, thus discrediting the father of all men, Jesus Christ. But the Bible gives men a clear path to make this right.

As men we want to control our own lives, but doing so keeps out both the control of God in our lives as well as our love for others. Whatever we love, we do not hold onto with gloves made of steel; we allow it to grow, take shape, blossom with life, and then, in the ultimate act of love, allow it to leave if it wants. If it chooses to come back, it is because it wants to, not because it has to.

Our need for control creeps up on us most often when life is going well, or when things generally seem to be getting better, and this applies to women and men both. "Well, that's better. Now, I can handle it," we think, and we jump in and dictate what to do next.

But that's when you stop doing what got you saved to begin with. You stop being involved in church and then you stop going to church altogether. Not long after that, you stop reading and praying as well. Then Christianity stops altogether, since your relationship with Christ ends when you stop asking him what to do. At that point, your primary goals have shifted away from Christ like living—staying connected with a body of believers, helping others, and constantly keeping your motives in check—and you are done for. Sin lie waiting for you just around the corner, and history, as it is bound to do, repeats itself.

Everyone thinks history is so boring, but if you look at it closely, you will find that much of what has gone on before is still happening today. Likewise, if you would look through your personal history, you'd see cyclical patterns. There are patterns in everything we do. Maybe you'd find that some times of the year were consistently tougher than others, or that certain situations were harder. Maybe certain people caused you more confusion and pain.

You could also see where you gave up and went back to old habits. Maybe something particular was going on in your life every time you slipped or someone specific was there. The key is to realize what was similar about your various backsliding episodes and then have enough brains and guts to say, "Hey, I need to avoid that, so it doesn't happen again. I've had enough of going around this mountain over and over, and I do not like to be miserable."

Without looking at your past, you will never understand your patterns; let alone what is at the root of them. And if you do not know your own history, you will repeat it. You won't know where you should be headed unless you sit down and look at where you've been. An added bonus of this process is that you will get to know yourself more intimately than you probably ever have, as you ask yourself questions such as, "When this happened, how did I react to it? When that happened, how did it change my life? What else and who else were in my life when I went through that? How am I doing and acting now, and how do my circumstances now compare to then?"

And then remember that regardless of all else, the best way to avoid the bad things from happening again is to consistently communicate with God and regularly attend church. God and church are where I get my serenity and my spiritually. And if I am seeking neither serenity nor spirituality, then I am seeking death. Think of death and life as two distinct ends. If you are seeking things in sin, you will meet death at the end, which means eternal separation from God. If you are seeking things in Christ, you will meet life.

As you start to learn more about where you've been and who you are, you will feel changed. Your heart will soften, and you will start to listen to others. You will learn to shoot up a prayer or two, or find time to meditate.

What was acceptable to you five weeks ago may not seem so acceptable now. And you will start to like who you are becoming. And when that happens, you want to change even more. The process continually gains momentum, until finally you are excited to go to church or your support group. You may also be surprised to find that others view you differently, maybe treating you more like a human being, and less like the plague, so you're excited to make friends. You're excited day after day because that is all you have—today. The change comes from inside and works its way out, encompassing all that goes with a life focused on Christ: respect, self-esteem, spirituality, and pure motives.

Friendships develop because we model who we admire. When we like what someone says, we check to see that their actions match their words, and if they do, we are attracted to them, and start modeling their behavior. But left to our own devices, the only behavior we know is sinful. Why? Because we are all born into sin, and many of us live with it too long. We need someone to teach us which behaviors to adopt to gain serenity in our lives.

We need to treat life with reverence, as it is a gift from God. We are here not only to try to get life right but to live it to its fullest. How? Jesus said that while we are here on earth, we are to keep the kingdom of God first, and then all other things will "be added unto you." This means that if I keep my relationship with Christ as the most important thing in my life, he will give me everything else that I could ever want and need, without my even trying.

You find your habits, interests, and attitudes changing. You start to put others first when you never did before. You start to want to do the right thing, and for no other reason than it is the right thing to do. The people you hang with change, as well as the things you do for enjoyment. And this change is the key to becoming and staying positive.

Fifteen: **Positive Attitudes**

Most people never get that success in life is directly due to two main things: whether your motives are pure and whether you are positive. And when I speak of being positive here, I do not mean a conditional feeling but a state of mind.

Most people also don't get the fact that life is a mindset, and so we must choose whether or not to be positive. In fact, the ability to recognize when you are not being positive is one of the greatest tools you will ever possess.

The reason some appear to be able to get past insurmountable odds in their lives is directly due to the fact that, instead of focusing on the negative, they look around to see what good things they can glean, from even the worst situations, in order to get to where they want to be.

When we get to points in our lives that seem to be sinkholes, places where everything appears dark and dismal, we need to be able to look up, ask God what is going on, and rely on him, knowing he will take care of us. After all, if we are going to trust God in the good times, we also need to trust him when it is darkest. When all things appear lost, and when it looks like there is no way out, there is always Jesus. He is the silver lining. Jesus is the one who allows us to be who we are in him. He is the one who gives us the courage to whistle in the dark and keep moving forward.

As such, the definition of courage as well as the definition of being positive is not the absence of fear or the absence of negativity; instead, it is the ability to trust in God and stay focused on him when we are feeling the most afraid and the darkest.

There will be times when we do not understand what is going on in our lives—times when we are doing the right things but still not getting to a point of seeing relief. We just have to feed the positive mindset and remember that there is always a reason. Jesus never does or allows anything for nothing. There is always a plan, and it is always for our betterment. We must continue to trust what he said when he stated that he would never leave or forsake us.

Jesus is positive, and his ways are positive. As mentioned in the previous chapter, he promises that we just have to seek him, and the things we need will be given to us. We do not have to go out and try to get them, or force our way on others, getting involved in the petty grievances of the world. We need only to keep our eyes focused on Christ.

The very fact that we have Jesus to rely on and to help us build positive thinking even in times of trouble suggests that a negative outlook is a byproduct of being of the world. When we do not know Christ personally, we think the way the world does; and as we all know, the world has a very negative view of things.

When we come from a place that is negative, everything we do is then negative. That's because we are starting with a foundation of negativity, and so everything built on it will be stilted. The world thrives on doom and gloom, and glorified negativity, as evidenced in the news.

When we commit ourselves to Christ and become new creatures, then, we must break out of that negative cycle and start down the positive path of Christ. And as we get practice looking at the positives, we change even more. This process takes time, of course, as we get so conditioned to being negative, but be patient with yourself, and a new outlook will come in time.

You will start to see life from a positive place to the point that others will even notice something different about you. That's because as you change and mature, your entire inside growth eventually becomes visible on the outside, manifesting itself in new, and positive perspectives.

This change takes effort, however. It would probably be easier to keep the same, negative outlook. As mentioned before, it takes someone special to stand firm in the higher calling that you have in Christ, to change and to view the world differently. But as hard as it may sometimes be, we have the certainty that with God, all things are possible. This is a precious gift that no one can take from us.

The Israelites had to go through the desert for forty years because they did not learn the lesson given them the first few times. They kept reverting back, time and again, to avoid the instruction they were to receive, so God kept them from the Holy land until the generation who would not learn had all gone. Let us not be like that. There is so much to be learned, so much to enjoy, and so much to partake of that going around the same mountain over and over is a waste. And with our new perspective, we can grasp the lesson being taught our first time through the valley, and move on. We learn from experience, trials, and tribulation, but once we get through, oh, the joy and life we will find on the other side. It is that learning process that we get maturation from. It is the going through that makes us who we are, not the avoiding.

Sixteen: Emotion vs. Truth

People get angry because of ego. For example, you usually get angry because something that someone said or did was not done to your satisfaction. As a result, you may get offended or have your feelings hurt. It really does not even matter what the circumstance is; the fact remains that since we do not always know how to use our feelings correctly, we turn the offense or hurt into anger.

Resentment starts as anger born out of insecurity. We become angry that we don't have it as good as someone else, and this anger feeds on itself until it grows into full-blown resentment.

Pity grows from anger that is born of hurt and then turned inward. Not able to work through our pain, we turn to pity, wanting everyone to feel sorry for us. Or, if that does not work, we feel sorry for ourselves. Then, everything we do comes from a place of depression. The problem with pity is that it separates us from the rest of the world. And, as such, pity becomes just another excuse. "No one has ever had it as bad as I do," we might say, or, "No one could possibly understand my situation." And thus we isolate ourselves from the rest of humankind, and excuse ourselves from negative behavior.

Once separated, the enemy can take us anywhere. This is why isolation is so dangerous—it traps us into unhealthy thinking about ourselves. We start to think that we are totally alone, or crazy, or just worse than everyone else, and if these thoughts are left alone to gain momentum, we may even begin to get ideas about ending it all, or just leaving it all behind. And if we stay too long in that place, the enemy knows horrible things will follow.

Be warned, however. As you make this transition, you may start to feel things that you are not used to feeling. Intense emotions, with regards to your life and salvation, may prompt you to think something is wrong. You may think, "This can't be right. I feel worse than I did before I asked Christ into my life." And this is the point where most people bail, if it does not occur to them to ask for help, or to just check with others to see whether their feelings are normal. That's said, because most of the time it's just that you are not experiencing or interpreting the emotions correctly, which is why, again, you often need a mentor to help you get through the first few months of salvation, or until you can get the intense feelings under control.

Anger is also usable against others. I actually can set myself up by having unrealistic expectations that others cannot possible live up to, so that when they fall short, I can slide right back into anger.

As with motives, positive and negative emotions cannot dwell in the same place simultaneously. The Bible states that it is impossible to serve two masters. In other words, it is not possible to have love and hate in your life at the same time, or serenity and anger, because these emotions exist at opposite poles. Therefore we need to choose what we will have in our lives. Do we want anger, resentment, and pity, or do we want happiness, love, and serenity? Because make no mistake about it, feelings are a choice.

Still, we all have buttons that, when pushed, get us going. So the trick is either to keep our buttons from getting pushed or, better yet, not have buttons in the first place. Buttons, after all, are nothing more than issues we have not resolved. They are those buried feelings that have not been dealt with, and so are triggered whenever a similar situation arises. How we deal with our emotions, then, will determine how many buttons we actually have, while how well we insulate ourselves will determine how often those buttons get pushed.

There is a theory that bias is created from emotions. The specific process in which this happens seems to work about the same for everyone. The idea is that what we think about something is determined by how we feel about it. So if we have a negative feeling about something that will color our judgment of it, and ultimately determine how we act toward it. (behavioral cognitive theory)If nothing else, this tells us that how we feel, think, and act is all tied together. And where do our emotions come from? The come from our perceptions of things, which is all based on how we were raised. Our feelings can dictate what we do, who we are acquainted with, and how we see things, and if not controlled, will get into every facet of our lives, ultimately leaving us in ruin.

Because of where our feelings can lead, we need to remember that they are not always accurate depictions of reality. Feelings are just sentiments—byproducts of our circumstances. And they can change on a dime so often that we cannot rely on them from moment to moment. All we need to do to change our feelings is to get away from the present situation, and, *voila*, they disappear, only to be replaced by new, different emotions. So the danger is in allowing our feelings to rule us, and control our behaviors. This is why the enemy wants us to live by emotions—he knows the minute we do, we are doomed.

So if we know that emotions are not stable, why do we give them so much credence? Why do they control us so much? And the most important question: how do we overcome them? We overcome feelings by not giving them a foundation in our lives.

As mentioned, feelings need someplace to go if not dealt with, otherwise they will negatively affect us. We need to learn to identify our feelings as we get them, so that we can ascertain how to deal with them. And if they are negative feelings, such as shame, hatred, envy, guilt, or remorse, we need to find out where they come from, work through them, and make amends with ourselves, as they do not play a part in a positive lifestyle.

Now this all is not to say that some feelings are not valid. Certain feelings can even keep us alive. If we feel fear in a dangerous situation and we act on it by getting out and staying safe, the feeling played a positive part in our life. The idea is just not to allow feelings to control us. So we need to asses each situation separately, determine how the feeling is affecting us, and then choose how to react. In other words, we need to strike a healthy balance between emotion and choice.

As we go through life, we attach emotions to different things. For each of us, certain sounds, smells, and tastes might have corresponding emotions attached to them. We need only to experience a sensation for a split second, and those associated feelings come flooding back. Take, for instance, a song that was playing when you broke up with your significant other in high school. To this very day, hearing that song on the radio can bring back the sadness you felt in that moment. We can actually go from being in a good place to feeling miserable in the time it takes a catch of scent something familiar in the air, and then get entangled in the past experience all over again. I believe this is a ploy by the enemy to recapture people who think they have dealt with emotions that they, in fact, have not.

That is how strong emotions can be if we allow them to go unchecked, which is why we need to be sure we have allowed Jesus to deliver us completely from our past. We can learn from our past, but we need not return to it, to relive it every time we feel a familiar sensation. If we do, we give the past power over us, and we give the emotion full reign over our being. So remember, not dealing with our feelings in the present is just prolonging process. In one ugly way or another, we will be faced with them later.

On the other hand, if you take the time that's necessary to deal with your emotions now, then in the end, it is over, never to haunt you again. In this way, dealing with feelings takes away both their power and the power of the situation that triggered them. I don't know about you, but I do not like anything to have power over me.

One good way to keep your emotions from controlling you is to get some distance from the triggering situation. Just hang back for a few before you commit yourself to a course of action, and think about things. You will find yourself in a much better place.

We also need to deal in truth, which is based in fact and not swayed by emotion. Christ states in his word that when we are living in him, we are living in truth. Truth is above emotion, because truth is not governed by circumstance. It is truth no matter what, where, why, or how. Truth does not depend on anything but itself; therefore, truth can stand alone. So, our choices are to live by truth and get it right, or live by emotion and have to go through the situation again later to get it right. We might as well just deal in truth from the start.

There is instability in living life based on feelings. Each feeling affects a person differently, and the same emotion affects various people differently, so there is not even stability in feelings themselves. I do not want to be ruled by my emotions. I want to be free to live my life as an offering to the Lord. I know I can be sure of myself at all times when I am ruled by truth—and because truth is from God, I am from God.

Christ is bound by truth. He will always deliver what he says he will. Therefore, if I put my trust in him, I can always be assured that the Word of God will operate in my life the way Jesus said it would. Letting my feelings determine how I act leaves too much room for the enemy to move in. I would much rather that the things that happen to me happen because Christ has put them in my life to help me grow.

As long as He is directing my footsteps, I will never fall or stumble. He guarantees that will never leave or forsake me, so I become his problem.

He will teach me how to deal with things as he would deal with them, which will always be the right way. I do not have to worry about anything, because he states that he has already determined my path. All I need to do is follow his word and do things his way, and all things will work out for good—even those things that the enemy tried to put in my path for the bad. All I need to do is believe that all of this is so, and he will get the glory.

Seventeen: **Just Stand**

There comes a time when everyone must choose to either fold or stand, usually when there is a battle going on, and usually when you feel your weakest. This is an attack from the enemy. I am at one such point in my life as I write this. There are so many fronts that are moving in, trying to steal my joy, and they have succeeded in enough areas that I am left feeling that one more incident will break me. I find myself sighing, breathing heavily at times, and just plain being depressed. It feels as though the energy has been sucked out of me, and what is left is just a shell.

I heard a famous preacher speaking on this exact thing this morning, and she stated that at these times, we must just trust in God, knowing that he will deliver us. But we must also know that it takes a mature Christian to hang in there and continue to do what is right even though everything around us is caving in. So, it is at these times that we are to just stand. Even as we experience one crisis after another, as life keeps handing us trouble, we are to just stand. Even if no one else is in sight, because they saw the writing on the wall and went running, you are to keep standing.

I have come to believe that hardship such as this happens to allow us to find out what we are made of. How much can we take? How far can you be pushed? Jesus already knows how you will react because he is God, but we do not, and neither does our family, so we have a horrid time.

Trouble is a proving ground for our faith. We get to choose how to react. Will we fall, or run screaming for the hills? Will we give it all up? Will we blame and curse God, whining about how everything sucks? Or will we go into his word, get to praying, and then, having done all we know how to do, just stand, waiting for Jesus to deliver us?

By blaming God, we fall into the trap of not believing that he can do what he said. By doubting, whining, getting depressed and angry, and, yes, even having thoughts of throwing in the towel, we, in essence, are saying that we can we can sail with Christ as long as the sea is calm, but when the going gets rough, we cannot handle it. We are showing that our faith is only good for the times when we are getting what we want, so, we are fair-weather friends of Christ, not true believers. There is a big difference.

If we truly believe that Jesus is who he said he is, and we have accepted him into our lives. And if we profess that he is in charge of our lives, then that should hold true no matter how things are going. Even if we lose everything and are abandoned by everyone, we are to stand. Paul states in Colossians, Ephesians, Corinthians, and Philippians that we are to put off the things of this world, and put on the things of Christ. And since we are no longer of this world, we are not to fall prey to the things of this world. Instead, we are to rise above and to trust Christ that all things work together for good to those who believe.

As mentioned, I am currently in one of those hard times, where I feel as though nothing is working the way I think it should. There are attacks every day, something that allows me to be pushed back into despair, into poverty, into desperation. So, to then read this stuff and try to believe it is increasingly hard. I feel as though I am walking in that valley of death and that the shadows are all out to get me. But I continue to stand, continue to write all of this in an attempt to clear my head, to get things out on paper, so that I can see them in front of me, figure out where I stand, and get things straight in my mind. Getting everything out also allows me to feel somewhat cleansed. I want to be able to believe. I want to stand firm. I want to be able to shrug off the things of this world and to move forward with Christ, paying no attention to what's around me. Because, ultimately, I know that Christ will deliver me—but so far I have this knowledge only in my head; getting it to my heart is another story.

I think that as we mature as Christians, we are faced with decisions that will direct the rest of our spiritual lives. How I choose to act when I am going through trials also determines what level of maturity I have. So these moments, I think, are where faith is built. They are decision points for our belief in Christ. We do not believe because that is just what happens; we must choose to believe. To have faith is to keep going through both the desert *and* the valley when you do not know how it is going to turn out. Meanwhile, if we have faith, and if we believe what we read in the Bible, we are reminded that we do know how it will turn out—that he will prevail. And since we are his kids, we too will prevail. He has told us to fear not, for he has overcome the world, and he has said that we are worth much more than flowers and wild animals, which he cares for, so how much more will he care for us, his children?

As I write, I start to see how much I have missed the mark. If I doubt, if I am unsure, if I am having trouble keeping joy, then I need to give those places over to Christ. The Bible states that I am not to worry, because what can my worrying change? If I am worrying, that is a place I need to give up to God. And if I trust in him, then I will not worry. I don't worry every time I go to turn on a light switch; I just have faith that the electric company is doing its job, and that the current will be there to make the thing work. I need to have the same faith in Christ.

If I profess that Jesus is my lord and that I believe his word is true, then I need let my actions demonstrate that. Regardless of how I feel, I need to walk in love. I need to forgive both others and myself, and I need not to keep score. I need to have faith that Christ is in the driver's seat and that everything that is happening in my life is happening for a reason. I do not have to know or like the reason; I just have to know that Jesus will not let me down.

Jesus has a plan for each of our lives, and that plan includes trials so that faith can have the chance to be exercised. Muscles that are not used begin to atrophy because they become useless, and that is exactly what would happen to our faith if we did not have a chance to put it to work. It is only when we get to use our faith that it grows. Every time we trust Jesus to help us work through a situation that previously baffled us, and he does, we have no doubt the next time we need him to work in that area.

This is where the mercy and grace that the Word speaks of comes into play. We need these two things daily because we often get into situations that we do not handle very well. Grace is what allows us to keep asking for forgiveness, while mercy is what allows Jesus to keep forgiving us. Grace is what gives us the opportunity to keep moving forward in Christ, as we continue getting caught up in ourselves. We may stand for a while, and then another problem hits us and we go into the pity mode, blaming God again. Grace is what allows us to repeatedly ask for forgiveness as we try to keep moving forward. Grace and mercy are the two things that allow us to stand. Without them, we are doomed.

It is very hard to put your trust in something that you cannot see, feel, touch, or hear. Even in the Old Testament, David said that he was not going to give God something that did not cost him anything. But every miracle that has been done has required some action on the part of the recipient. So while we can do nothing to earn grace and mercy, we still have to let God work in us to give up our old lives, our old ways, and the unacceptable things we used to do.

It hurts to have our flesh ripped from us. It is painful to undergo an operation by a spiritual scalpel. Yet, to be rid of our flesh is the only way for us to truly get right with Christ. For that to happen, he must get into our lives, and cut away all of the dead parts of us, to make room for the new.

In gardening terms, this process is called pruning. To produce good, healthy fruit, plants must be pruned. If they are not, the excess branches suck up most of the energy and nutrients, leaving little for the tree to use to produce fruit. As a result, whatever fruit does grow is underdeveloped and unhealthy. We, as Christians, must also produce fruit, but if we are not pruned every once in a while, then how can we produce healthy sustenance to help others? We can't. Therefore, Christ must sometimes allow us to be in a position where he can cut away at those things which are not bearing fruit. And this is painful.

The spiritual axiom is that the more of ourselves we give to Christ, the more freedom we get in return. So the more we realize that we are not in the driver's seat any longer, and that now Christ is directing our lives, the easier it will be to get through trials. Our flesh is in constant confrontation with the spirit. This is what the Word was speaking of when it said that we have to die to self or die to the flesh. Our will does not want to go softly into that good sleep. It wants what it wants right now, which consequently is what got us into this mess to begin with.

Right now, I am experiencing many situations in my life that I really have no control over. I feel overwhelmed, and like I have been dragged through the streets for a mile or so, at fifty miles per hour, and without a shirt. I have been whining, complaining, feeling sorry for myself, and, yes, blaming God on and off for about a few months now. Jesus has been trying to prune me to allow for new growth, but I feel pain is all I'm getting from it so far. I have been going back and forth among asking for help, blaming, hating, and asking for forgiveness, all while trying to stay faithful to him. In Colossians, it says that we should feel grateful for being disciplined; I guess I am not that mature yet, as all I feel is pain. But as I continue to write, I get glimpses here and there of understanding, and I think I am beginning to learn what he is trying to teach me.

I have always relied on myself. I have always had an out, a backup plan. I have always found an angle, but not this time. I am actually out of things to try. I have been placed in a situation that I now have to trust in Jesus, and only Jesus, to get me through, as there appears to be no other way. That means that my flesh has to die, and my ways must go with it, so there is pain. I get scared when I am not in control. I do not trust or have faith easily. I also do not know what it means to have a father who loves me, who cares about me, or who wants to take part in my life. So having to trust in a heavenly father who I can't reach, touch, see, feel, or hear is quite unsettling and, quite frankly, hard to do. Unfortunately, it is necessary to do if I want to get to the next level and mature in Christ.

God, I think, cannot forever leave you where you are and use you. There has to be growth and maturation, or you would be ineffective for doing battle with the enemy. The devil would hit you with something, and because you knew no better, you would fall for it, thus letting him win.

Plus, no relationship is static; growth is necessary. Likewise, a walk with Christ is dynamic; it has a life of its own, and it sometimes takes all we have to keep up with the things he has to teach us. That is why the Word of God, as well as not forsaking the fellowship of believers, is so necessary. These two areas are where we can come together and compare notes, and help uplift one another in times of need. None of us can do this alone.

Jesus wants us to rely on him; our flesh wants us to rely on ourselves. Our flesh has only one goal, and that is to please itself. Jesus has only one goal, as well, and that is to love. To love is selfless, but the flesh is selfish. To love is to keep no record; the flesh keeps score. To love is to place others before ourselves; the flesh states that we are the most important person, and to hell with others. Love states that we should give of everything we have; the flesh states that we should take what we can get, and then try to get more.

All I really want is to be successful, to have the ability to help others, to love unconditionally, and to hear from God. (By that, I mean to not have to guess, but to be certain that God spoke to me.) Sometimes, I think I hear from God, but it turns out to be my just hearing what, at the time, I wanted to hear. One TV preacher I heard once said that he had conversations with God. He said that he actually hears from God and is God's friend. I would really like that. I would like to have a running conversation with God, and feel as though he were right there with me, right in the same room, that he could hear me and I could hear him. There would be no guessing, no doubt, and a certainty that he and I were friends. We would talk about his stuff and about my stuff. I mean, surely God has things to talk about; after all, he became human for a time. He knows what it is to need a friend, to need to talk, and to need to dump stuff. I do believe that that kind of relationship is possible with him.

What we are attached to is different for all of us, but we are all attached to something or another. Usually, they are things that our flesh believes we can't do without and thus the things that are the most difficult to give up. We all create habits in our lives that become so ingrained in us that we do them by force of habit, without a thought. And this reality is never as evident as when we are tested. On the surface, we want to give Jesus whatever he wants, but there are those few things that we hold off to one side. Some of those things are hidden in our hearts so deep that at times we do not even know they are there or what harm they are doing. These are the things that God wishes to remove. They are our pets, our safeguards. But God. God knows when we are ready to let go. He knows when to push and when to back off. If only we could learn more easily.

I know for me, I need to learn balance and consistency. I need to have balance in my life so that all things complement each other and I can become well-rounded. And as for consistency, that is the key to change that lasts. If I can be consistent in all things, knowing that if this happens, I will do that, and if that happens, I will do this every time, then life would be simpler. Instead, probably like most, I tend to complicate things by always trying to change things up, usually to find an easier way. But that is when things go south. All things must go through him, and there is no easier way. If I knew how to be consistent, I would directly go to prayer instead of into panic mode every time life got to me. If life threw me a curve, and balance ruled, I would not get so upset; I would just know that I trust God to provide a way. I would remember is that only the footwork is up to me. The result is up to God.

The war between flesh and spirit has been going on for as long as there has been flesh. Adam and Eve were in a place where all their needs were taken care of. They were able to walk with God, talk with God, interact with God face to face, but that was not good enough for flesh. The enemy knew this because the enemy is flesh. So, he made them an offer that their flesh could not turn down. Their spirit could have, but because they were not operating in the spirit all the time, they were deceived.

Eve's issue was that she listened to an abomination in the first place. Why did she not call out to God as soon as the serpent made a sound? Why did she listen at all? Then why did she lie about what God had told her? And, ultimately, why did she eat of the fruit that was forbidden? If she knew nothing about the difference between good and evil, why did she want to? What did she think they were missing?

Adam was no better. He was right beside his wife, listening to the whole conversation. In fact, as head of the home, he was more responsible to stop the conversation than she was. And he was made in the image of God, with no flaws, defects, or imperfections, so just what did he think knowledge of good and evil would do for him? If God had wanted Adam to have it, he would have given it to him from the start.

All of this couple's wants and needs were dealt with by God himself, so all they would have to do was call upon him. He would have come and put the devil in his place then, before it was too late. Yet, this is still what happens to us today. We think we are missing something, something more we do not know, so we look further than we need to, just to find something we usually had no business with in the first place. The lust of the flesh is a terrible thing.

And all this is not to mention that Adam had power. When God had included Adam in the creation process, he gave him the ability to have authority and dominion over everything else lower than him, which was everything on earth. So Adam had the power to take authority over the serpent, rebuke it, and remove its existence. This fact makes his sin almost doubly bad, because he could have stopped the whole thing right there.

But as we all know it did not go that way. Instead, all power was given over to the enemy. And from that time until Christ sacrificed himself on the cross, we had nothing—no birthright, no power, no dominion, and no authority. Of course, all of that changed with Christ, but sometimes we act like it didn't. We still choose to live in the bondage of sin. We still listen to deception. We still allow the enemy to speak to us.

At least, I know I do. Because after writing nine pages now, it has been revealed to me that the whole reason I am in turmoil is because I still have not learned to stop listening to the enemy. It has dawned on me that I am a child of God. I, like Adam, have power and dominion, and the authority to change things through prayer. I have the ability to affect change in my life by taking authority over the circumstances and living in truth, balance, and consistency.

Now I understand what the Word of God means when it says that we choose blessings or curses, life or death. We have the choice to use our authority, our dominion, to defeat the enemy in battle. I can choose to listen to the Word of God or to the enemy. Jesus gave us back what Adam gave away.

So, if I choose to listen to the negative garbage that is whispered in my ear, or if I choose to live by the reality I see in front of me instead of believing what I read in the Word, then that is what I will get. It has to be this way because of free will. God will not force us to live a certain way. He will not intervene in a situation to which he is not invited. So by allowing us to go through turmoil, Jesus is giving us the chance to use the authority he has given us. By giving us the opportunity to exercise our free will, he is giving us the chance to grow in Him.

This is where I have failed. I have been too consumed with what is going on around me, to worried about the physical realities, that I have not though just to trust in the Word of God. I allowed the enemy a place in my life by listening to him, which has caused confusion, doubt, and ineffectiveness, and which drawn to its conclusion could equal sin and death. However, I do not believe that I am the only one this happens to, so I hope this revelation can inspire others in similar situations.

So this is what it means to stand. After doing all you know how to do, just keep standing, and Christ will honor that. He knows what you can handle. He knows just how far you can go in any one setting. But, it is up to you to go and get your victory. It is not just going to be handed to you. Just as with miracles, you have to go and get the victory. It is yours for the taking; you just have to say the Word and stand.

As I write more and more, these truths are settling in and becoming more personal. I see how they apply to my life circumstances. I want all that I can have. I want prosperity in every area I am entitled to. And I want balance, continuity, and consistency in my life all the time. The real chore is to hate the way you are feeling, then having the wisdom to change it without ruining all that is in your life.

Flesh is a prideful thing, and it will not give up easily—not without a fight. And since we have been doing things from our flesh for most of our lives, let's face it: when we deny it, it is going to scream bloody murder. Luckily, in the end, Jesus knows where we need to go and what we need to do to win the battle. His vision for us is clear, while ours is cloudy. We must just stand firm, try to see past the here and now, and find the big picture.

Eighteen: Condemnation vs. Conviction

Condemnation and conviction; there is a big difference between these two, as one is from above and one is from below.

Condemnation is always from the enemy, as it is always negative in nature. Condemnation never helps, and always hurts. It never has positive results, but will drag us down and bring us to a point of desperation. Condemnation is like a cancer; it eats away at us, undermining all that we do and all that we are. It will attack us at our most vulnerable point and then invade every area of our life, completely taking over. Its nature is to undermine all that the Holy Spirit has done. It is a tool of the enemy, and its only purpose is to kill and destroy.

Condemnation is always going to take from you. It will take your serenity, happiness, and peace. And the only things it will give you in return are resentment, anger, and guilt, or shame. There is nothing the enemy gives without requiring something in return. At first, the price might not appear that high, but after closer inspection, you find hidden costs that you had not seen before. With the enemy, nothing is totally up-front; there is always a back end.

Conviction is the opposite of condemnation. With conviction, there is a feeling of love, a kind of gentle swaying toward forgiveness. Conviction does not give a sense of self-loathing. Instead, it softly nudges us away from the wrong path and toward the right one. It then helps us to get back on strong footing, allowing us to see how we went wrong, and to make things right with God and others. Conviction teaches and always leads to a positive end.

With condemnation, we feel guilty for everything we do. But in (Romans 8: 1–2, NIV) Paul states clearly that "there is now no condemnation for those in Christ Jesus, because through Christ Jesus, the law of the spirit of life set me free from the law of sin and death." You see, because of Jesus, we are free from the death sentence associated with a life of sin, so there is no need for condemnation.

Condemnation separates us from God in a very seductive way. It places within us the feeling that we do not measure up, or that, somehow, we are not good enough to be in Christ. It is performance-based Christianity's best tool for getting us to do what religion wants us to do. It ushers in guilt, shame, and remorse, and sets us up to be less-than. It places us in a position to always want to do more to prove ourselves, and it requires us to do more work to earn forgiveness—when in reality, Jesus already paid the penalty of sin for us on the cross.

As we try to work through feelings of condemnation, which is an impossible task, we ultimately become frustrated and, in the end, resentful of the Christian life. We start to ask ourselves if this whole thing is really worth it, and, of course, the answer is usually no.

Conviction shows us a better way to get through something. When we are being convicted, it is usually because the Holy Spirit is trying to get us to see things another way. Conviction is about changing direction. It will always lift us up and offer an option for what to do next. It is usually gentle, and may come in the form of correction from a loved one or from that small, still voice that says, "Isn't there a better way to do this?" or, "Do you really need to be involved with that?" or, "Is this leading you on the path to life?" Conviction offers a better way to handle a situation, a way that is usually more pleasing to God while also being more beneficial to us.

Nineteen: Performance-Based Christianity

There are two types of relationships we can have with Christ. The first is the proper one, based on Jesus' mercy, grace, and unmerited favor. The second is just the opposite and what I call performance-based Christianity, better known as religion. Most people who grow up in dysfunctional homes or churches end up in the second type. But a performance-based relationship is unbiblical because it says we can earn God's favor with our own effort. Isaiah 64:6 states that all of us have become like those who are unclean and that all our righteous acts are as filthy rags, so even our best efforts fall short of giving us eternal life. It is only through God's grace and mercy, not effort, that we are right with God.

As fallible humans, we need God to meet us where we are and provide us the means to release ourselves to him. Then only through his power are we transformed. But, how exactly do we let go? First, realizing that we can achieve nothing on our own, the first step is to stop trying. The second step is to pray for help in truly allowing him into every area of our lives, since, remember, if we hold on to anything from our past, the enemy uses it against us.

I have tried to find loopholes—ways to keep some things and let others go, but in the end, I have found that without total surrender, it is not possible to be right with God. There is no such thing as a half-sin or a little sickness. The phrase "One bad apple can spoil the whole basket" is true. Once we allow a little compromise into our behavior, it sets the standard for all future behaviors, and at the end of that compromise is sin and death. But, this is the spiritual axiom: with surrender comes power. Once we let our old selves go, Christ can then come into our lives and transform us into his image—and that, indeed, is not a bad image to have.

It is the willingness to completely let go of our old selves that allows Christ to come in and start to work. And Jesus does this work—not us—nudging us with conviction and that small, still voice within our consciences.

We have to do some footwork, though; this much we can do. In the Bible, for every miracle performed, the person receiving it had to do the footwork, and that is still what happens today. Things like going to church, Bible studies, and prayer meetings; praying and allowing God to move in our lives; and meditating on the Word all lay the groundwork for miraculous changes in us. (In fact, I have found that when I speak the word out loud, changes come quicker. The spoken word has great power and can affect change. In Genesis, we see that the whole world was spoken into existence.)

Surrender doesn't only happen at the beginning of our relationship with Christ, either. We must choose to die to self daily. We must deny ourselves the sins we used to do and enjoy, exchanging them for righteousness and freedom each day. And we must follow the Word of God and allow its words into our hearts and consciences.

By learning to stop trying with our own power and allowing God to step in, we must give ourselves completely over to him. And only then can his will for us take root. So, how did we get so misguided? The fault lies with many of our former role models. Those who thought nothing was ever good enough and allowed us to think that we were second-class citizens because we could not measure up to their unrealistic expectations. These people left us in a jam, leading us to believe that if only we tried harder, if only we'd give that one last ounce of effort, it might finally be good enough, only to find once again that we had fallen short. To have our goals smashed and our dreams crushed, and to be made to feel as though we were worthless yet again was devastating to our spiritual growth.

But no matter what we did, it would never measure up, because in reality they were not looking at us with that disdain in their eyes; whether they knew it or not, they were actually looking in the mirror, feeling how much they had disappointed themselves and others. Perpetually angry and resentful, they found it easier to take out their negative feelings on us. We could not defend ourselves, we believed them, and then we were crushed, but by making us miserable, they felt better about themselves. Because they were not the people they envisioned themselves to be, and never would be, they got even with life by taking ours early, thus absolving themselves of guilt and shame—at least outwardly. But inwardly, they became further separated from themselves, and the more miserable they became, the more pain they inflicted. Hurt people hurt people. And by producing little disenfranchised people, they perpetuate the cycle of hurt.

Ultimately, we will either give up our futile efforts and turn to a life of sin or learn that with Christ, it is not what we do that makes him love us, because he has always loved us. From the creation of the universe, he stated that he has known us; he knit us together in the womb. And he loves us because that is just what he does.

Behavior-based Christianity can take many faces. Not being able to say no, for example, even if we are overwhelmed, out of fear that the person asking will not like us, be disappointed in us, or just not hang out with us anymore. For those of us who are dependent on others' approval to feel loved or worthy, saying no is downright unacceptable. It does not even occur to us that people might like us because of who we are. We think that people will only like us for what we can accomplish and provide, which, in turn, means we feel valuable only in terms of what we can do.

With this frame of mind, we come up with this elaborate system of Christianity, believing that God rewards us for what or how much we allow him to work in our lives. Instead of just accepting ourselves and allowing him to work, we struggle with everything he offers. We slave within ourselves, always seeking his favor by doing more or allowing him to work more. Or, when we want Christ to do something for us, we perform these elaborate acts that we feel God should rubber-stamp.

Thus, we get into a habit of believing that Jesus will do what we want because of how much we do for him or how much we let him do in us. We base every action on action. But by doing so, we put ourselves, rather than God, at the helm of the relationship.

And when God does not come through the way we expect, we become disappointed and eventually resentful toward God for not giving us what we wanted. It becomes a very nasty cycle of negativity. We are never fully happy with what is going on in our lives. It is not possible, because something is always missing. We have never done enough, or Jesus did not respond the way we expected. Regardless, we are left wanting. We forget that God is sovereign, that Jesus will do for us because he loves us, and that we do not have to do a thing to be noticed and cared for. He knows what and how we are doing every moment, as well as what we are going to do. Otherwise, he would not be God; he would be Steve, Bob, or Joe.

Paul states in Hebrews that a life with Christ is a blood-bought covenant that originated with Abraham and Sarah and was fulfilled with Jesus. We have the birthright that comes with being adopted into the Christ lineage. We are, by birth, rightful partakers in the covenant with Christ. When we gave our hearts to him and were baptized in water, we became "new creatures in Christ, old things have passed away, and behold, all things are new." This is a free gift; it cannot be earned. It is the epitome of mercy and grace in action. Once we get this, we move from performance-based Christianity to true Christianity, founded in grace, mercy, and unmerited favor.

This is a hard step for many. Some of us have been going around the same mountain for so long that we have dug ourselves into a groove in the ground. We have gotten stuck in a pattern, locked into a certain way of living that will not allow us to change. We are like the Israelites coming out of slavery. Back in Egypt, the Israelites, as slaves, had been constantly told what to do. They were told when to eat, when to sleep, what to think, and how to act to the point that they became unable to do anything for themselves. They longed for freedom.

But once given that freedom by God, through Moses, they were lost. They were totally unprepared for life without masters. As they made their trek across the desert to the promise land, they continually grumbled, whined, and complained, always one step from turning around and going back to Egypt. To them, it seemed easier to go back and do what they were told than to have to think for themselves and move to a place where they would have to relearn how to live through God—even though it meant having a better quality of life and being free from oppression.

We are like that. When we come to Christ, we do not know how to live freely, so we resist all efforts by Christ to change us. We have been slaves to sin for so long, that all we can do is grumble and threaten to go back. When we don't see results right away, we tell everyone that this God stuff really does not work and, sometimes, we may even quit. If we were really honest, we would tell them, instead, that we did not really give our new life a fair chance—we were too afraid.

So we need to be able to start from scratch. We need to admit that we don't have a clue about how to live freely. Then God can work. He can re-educate us to believe in his way of life, based on grace, mercy, and unmerited favor, and he can restore us to the place in which he intended us to be: in power, and all because we have what he died to give us.

This is the ultimate goal. Christ died to give us freedom in him, and to be one with him in glory, starting here on earth and finishing in heaven. He was the sacrifice for us; we were not the sacrifice for him. On the cross, Jesus forever put to rest our need to make a sacrifice in return for his forgiveness.

Afterword

Addiction is addiction, no matter what the cause. We can become addicted to almost anything. If we have an addictive personality, however, we need to take special care of what we do.

Some prescription medications, once started, need to be taken continually, with no exception, which means that if you cannot get a refill at the pharmacy right away after your previous batch is gone, or if your doctor decides to take you off of it for a while, you go into withdrawal. I would not wish withdrawal on my worst enemy. It is like having the flu, only intensified by about 100 percent, for over a week. It is a horrible thing to have to go through, especially when you are already in pain.

If anyone reading this is a chronic-pain patient, I understand what you are going through. That is why I want to assure you that there are places out there that can help; the Internet is a good place to start searching. Also be assured that you are not crazy, that it is not all in your mind, and that eventually, it will all come out in the wash. The doctors will find something that is causing your pain, so just hang in there. Do not give up.

I also know how hard it can be not to take more medication than you are supposed to. But when you are in pain, and you have access to pain medication, just taking the medication when you hurt is unacceptable. You must take the doses as prescribed. If you need more, talk to your doctor or a support group, but do not make the mistake I did and try to self-medicate.

There was a brief time in my life where I was on Oxycontin. Let me just state right here and now that, in my opinion, this drug has got to be one of the worst on the market today. It almost drove me to do things that I would not have even considered doing at any other time. Highly addictive, this drug also took over my life to the point that I started looking for other places to get it. I was already receiving the script for it from my regular doctor, but I found another one on Long Island who would prescribe it to me, as well. I ended up taking twice the medication I should have. Every two weeks, I found myself driving four hours each way just to get a second prescription. This lasted about eight or nine months, until, by the grace of God, I was sent to another doctor who switched me to a less-addictive drug called MS Contin, at which point the addiction issues went away literally overnight.

The key is not to keep any medication your taking a secret. I am sure you have heard the saying "We are only as sick as our secrets." Well, I have found that to be true. If we talk about what is going on in our lives with others, and we are open about our issues, they do not have a chance to overtake us. You may be surprised at how many others you find going through similar issues; it's just that everyone is afraid of being judged or ridiculed or talked about. So it usually ends up better for everyone for you to talk. Besides, it would not be worth it to die or become trapped in addiction because you were afraid to talk.